STUDY AND COMMENTARY ON
THE FRUIT OF THE SPIRIT

Fruit

OF THE

Vine

Dr. Lee Ann B. Marino, Ph.D., D.Min., D.D.

Fruit of the Vine

STUDY AND COMMENTARY ON THE FRUIT OF THE SPIRIT

Dr. Lee Ann B. Marino, Ph.D., D.Min., DD.

Published by:
Righteous Pen Publications
(The Righteousness of God shall guide my pen)
www.righteouspenpublications.com

All rights reserved. Except as permitted under the U.S. Copyright Act of 1976, no part of this book may be reproduced, distributed, or transmitted in any form or by any means, electronic or mechanical, or saved in any information storage and retrieval system without written permission from the author.

Unless otherwise noted, Scriptures taken from the Holy Bible, New International Version ®, NIV®, Copyright © 1973, 1978, 1984, 2011 by Biblica, Inc.™ Used by permission of Zondervan. All rights reserved worldwide.

Passages marked KJV are from the King James Version of the Holy Bible, Public domain.

All word definitions are from ***Strong's Exhaustive Concordance of the Bible*** by James Strong, STD., LL.D., Public domain.

Cover and interior photos are in the public domain, Pexels.com: Dilara (cover) and Kelian Pfleger (chapters).

Book classification:
1. Books > Religion & Spirituality > Christian Books & Bibles > Christian Living.

Copyright © 2015, 2024 by Dr. Lee Ann B. Marino.

ISBN: 1940197260
13-Digit: 978-1-940197-26-5

Printed in the United States of America.

Acknowledgements

There are so many who have done so much to help me develop the fruit of the Spirit in my own life. To all of them, I am very grateful, especially to those ministers and ministries that have displayed the true fruit of the Spirit to me over the years. I am grateful for the different leaders who taught me, instructed me, and helped me along. I am so grateful to the many ministries who have opened their pulpits to me, especially in realization that this ministry is not quite like any other. In taking a chance on a different minister, you opened a world of truth and hospitality to me and those who travel with me. Even if we are no longer in contact at this time, I am still grateful for the role you played in my life.

At this point, I am also truly indebted to all who have helped equip the work of Spitfire Apostolic Ministries, especially in the plant of Sanctuary International Fellowship Tabernacle – SIFT. I also thank our friends, partners, podcast listeners, and those who believe in us, everywhere in the world.

Lastly, I thank you, the reader, who has purchased a copy of this book because you desire to bear more excellent fruit in your life. May this book bring you to a place where you are better prepared and graced to stand with the fruit of the vine present in your own life.

Table of Contents

    Introduction... 1

1 The Fruit of the Spirit... 9

2 Love.. 25

3 Joy.. 47

4 Peace.. 67

5 Patience (Long-Suffering, Forbearance)...................... 89

6 Kindness... 111

7 Goodness.. 131

8 Faithfulness.. 153

9 Gentleness (Humility)... 177

10 Self-Control.. 197

11 Conclusion: Harvest-Time Reflections..................... 219

    About The Author... 225

Introduction

But the fruit of the Spirit is love, joy, peace,
forbearance, kindness, goodness, faithfulness, gentleness
and self-control.
Against such things there is no law.
- Galatians 5:22-23

I am not an agricultural person. I don't like the country. It's full of bugs and snakes and small towns that remind me too much of Mayberry on the *Andy Griffith Show*. You know the kind of places I am talking about: they are the ones where nothing is ever going on, thus people are forced to hang out at the barber shop…or the corner store…or worse, the local gas station (that doesn't even have a public restroom). I love cities, tall buildings, concrete under my feet, museums, life, and the energy of urban areas. I have never, to date, been on a working agricultural farm. The closest I ever got was a school trip to a maple syrup farm when I was in second grade. (The only thing interesting about that trip was the maple sugar candy.) Everyone who knows me knows I love plants (especially rosebushes), but I've learned to put a cap on that interest because they require things like time and attention. The eternal threesome of ministry, work, and marriage don't always afford me the time for many hobbies, thus I must limit the number of plants I have to those I can reasonably keep alive. I think agriculture is good work…noble work…and important work…but I know it's not what I am called to do.

While I might be a person destined for the city, I can't escape the fact that the Bible was written in an agricultural culture. Its authors lived in a time when most people were very connected to agrarian society for survival's sake. That's why so much of the Bible is written in agricultural terms. The people of old understood about times and seasons, seed time and harvest, sowing and reaping, and all those other good terms that we throw around today without a whole lot of understanding. They weren't preoccupied with computers, the internet, getting people to like you on social media, or trying to generate a multitude of followers. People were a little simpler then, just trying to survive. That is why the analogies made to agricultural systems in the Bible were so poignant: people would associate Biblical principles not as a mere option, but as means of spiritual survival.

So, when we started talking about fruit and vines and excellent fruit in an organization I used to belong to, I started wondering what exactly we were talking about. Yeah, I knew what fruit was and I understood that grapes grew on vines, but what exactly does it mean to be in the "fruit of the Spirit?" Sure, it sounds all great and poetic to talk about being "in the vine" and about "bearing fruit," but hearing these passages in so many modern contexts for so many years left me a little curious. Often, we hear preachers talk about agricultural things in terms of money, and it's tempting to assess ourselves a little too materialistically when it comes to spiritual things. It's great to reap a financial blessing, but we all know plenty of people who grace the pews of the church every week with lots of money and their matching outfit from hat to suit to shoes to handbag…who, let's just say…leave a bit to be desired in the "spiritual fruit" area. There are people who have every material thing we dream of having and want, and they are completely void of spiritual character.

The truth about spiritual fruit is that it has nothing to do with money. It has nothing to do with our income, because the Bible says that He sends rain on the righteous and the unrighteous alike (Matthew 5:45). People who have lots of money can have great character, but they can also have lousy character. Poor people can have great character or lousy character. The measure of our spiritual fruit, of how much we have taken hold of spiritual virtues in our lives, is not reflected in how much "stuff" we have. The sooner we realize this, the better off we will be. God wants to do something within each one of us that has nothing to do with money, and it's something that none of us can go out and buy in the store. We can all have it if we will work with Him, and it won't cost us a thing. No matter how much or how little we have, we can all have it. He desires us to develop fruit and develop more excellent fruit (John 15:2). The question becomes, how do we do this?

Let's first understand that in agriculture, there is a process involved in fruit production. It's easy for city folk like myself to assume that someone just plants a tree and it does its thing, but that's far from the truth. Whether fruit grows on a tree, a vine, or a bush, a farmer spends many years developing their craft of bringing forth the best quality fruit possible. For this book specifically, I did some research into grape production. When God spoke to me about this book, I saw the importance of understanding fruit production as relates to the vine, because Jesus told us that He is the vine, and we are the branches (John 15:5). I selected grapes because they are used so frequently throughout the Bible to illustrate different points. Likewise, the principals involved in grape production are so vitally important for us as believers.

It turns out that grape cultivation is thousands of years old and considered a time-honored art form. They don't just throw some seeds into the ground and hope for the best. Grape cultivators must consider everything from climate and temperature to soil pH, water, and pest control. They must monitor their plants carefully to tell if there are any problems. Cultivators constantly check leaves, vines, stems, and soil to make sure the vineyard will bring forth the best of the best, no questions asked. Once the grape berries begin to form in clusters, the fruit is inspected to make sure it is growing properly. Even after harvest time, grape cultivators consider what they will do with their grapes. Not all grapes wind up in the market in the form of fresh fruit. Wine production is an entirely different art form, as is the pressing of grapes to make juice, or drying grapes to make raisins. With fruit production at such a premium, why would God tell us to produce fruit if it is such a long and complicated process?

Because it's such a long and complicated process. That's the point. It takes time to get great fruit in the natural, and it also takes time for us to get great fruit in the spiritual. We don't just wake up one day and suddenly bear spiritual fruit. It's a discipline that requires time, effort, cultivation, and deliberate intention as we go through our walk of faith and learn new things about God and ourselves along the way.

God never promised us that being in faith was going to be easy. That's the part of faith that I think we don't like to talk about today. The church today in general (not everyone specifically) likes the idea of measuring things quickly and on the surface. If a tree or a vine has a few buds, they like to think of that as adequate fruit. This is not, however, what God has asked of us! Every single one of us is called to put in some time and effort when we walk in faith. This book is about the fruit of those efforts, what they should look like, and what we should come to see when we walk in the fruit of the Spirit.

This book is not just about what the fruit of the Spirit might be in theory, but about how it looks, what it becomes, and about thinking about the fruit in your own life. It's meant to serve as a tool and a thinking point, one that helps you assess your own spiritual fruit a little bit better. I am classifying this as a "study devotional" because it is written to identify and ponder at the same time. Throughout the study, you will notice some important points to consider that go along with the text. In keeping with our fruit theme, they all have themes that relate to grape production. These are:

- **Bud Breaks**: Bud breaks are when the growth cycle of grapes begins. They are the first signs that grape production has started. Our word studies throughout this book are called "bud breaks" because learning and understanding these words helps us start understanding more about how their attributes manifest in our lives. You need to know these words to understand the fruit of the Spirit better.

- **Pruning Points**: Grape vines need to be pruned according to a specific method that will help the vine to grow and flourish during growing season. Pruning is typically done when the vine is dormant, usually in late winter right before spring comes. The goal of pruning is to cut off the old vines that are no longer fruitful or producing fruit, because they take nutrients away from new, flourishing plants. When we are told to prune spiritually, it is to cut off dead, dying things in our lives that are hampering our development of fruit. These may be any variety of things…so be prepared for some points on areas in your lives that need pruning.

- **Power Pollination**: Grapes vary in their pollination methods. Some grape plants are male or female, and others are hermaphroditic, which means that they have both male and female characteristics in one plant (these can self-pollinate!) Honeybees do not contribute to grape pollination. Instead, these plants pollinate through the wind. Pollen is carried via breeze from one point to another. We know the Spirit is often compared to the wind (John 3:8), and when we are in fruit production, the residue of our "pollen" should blow to other plants (believers) and affect the vine in bigger ways. These points help you to learn how to spread the fruit of the Spirit to others.

- **Foundational Fertilizer**: Grapes require fertilizer in addition to good sun and good soil. The secret with fertilizing grapes is to make sure you don't fertilize too much or too little. In our study, I am fertilizing your experience with stories from my own experiences with the fruit of the Spirit. Just because I am writing a book on it doesn't mean I am the "master" of the fruit of the Spirit; quite the contrary, in fact. I am walking through this faith walk just like you are and am learning a lot about myself as God reveals to me about these matters, too. Laugh, cry, or study along as I try to offer just enough – not too much or too little – to keep you encouraged in this process and realize you are not alone as you deal with your own faults and the faults of others!

- **Happy Harvest**: Many teach "harvest" to be the end of the process. It is, in reality, the beginning of something else. Once you harvest your crop, you must do something with it! In the case of grapes, they either become fresh fruit, raisins, wine, or ingredients for cooked or baked items. Harvest is a new beginning! Amid your happy harvest, here are some things for you to do with your harvest!

Each chapter also opens with three assignments. One is a reading assignment related to that aspect of the fruit of the Spirit that we are studying in that chapter, and the other two activities are to help you develop more "excellent fruit" in the specific aspect of that chapter's study.

Over the next several days, let's let God speak to us about our fruit…how we can develop it…make it more excellent…and wow the world with our harvest. With insights, some humor, a little warmth, and a good dose of fruit, full to the brim, the fruit of the

Spirit is waiting for us all to partake of it – and its Leader – in a greater dose...including me, too.

Chapter One

The Fruit of the Spirit

"I AM THE TRUE VINE, AND MY FATHER IS THE GARDENER.
HE CUTS OFF EVERY BRANCH IN ME THAT BEARS NO FRUIT,
WHILE EVERY BRANCH THAT DOES BEAR FRUIT HE PRUNES
SO THAT IT WILL BE EVEN MORE FRUITFUL.
YOU ARE ALREADY CLEAN BECAUSE OF THE WORD
I HAVE SPOKEN TO YOU. REMAIN IN ME, AS I ALSO REMAIN IN YOU.
NO BRANCH CAN BEAR FRUIT BY ITSELF; IT MUST REMAIN
IN THE VINE. NEITHER CAN YOU BEAR FRUIT
UNLESS YOU REMAIN IN ME."
— JOHN 15:1-4

Assignments:
- Read Galatians 5:16-26.
- Eat an orange or other multi-sectional fruit and ponder the concept of many parts in one unit.
- Think of areas for self-improvement where sin is dominant in your life.

The fruit of the Spirit has never been the most popular topic for preaching. In my many years of ministry, I recall one message on the fruit of the Spirit. I saw it on television so long ago, I don't remember much about it. It didn't speak to me in the way it should have, because from what I do remember about it, things about money and having money were littered in between its contents. Rather than being about real character, it was a way to use the spiritual system to get what you wanted out of it. Somehow, looking back, I don't think that's what God wanted us to get out of learning about the fruit of the Spirit.

Then there was the time that I went to a women's meeting at a church with the meeting theme being, "the fruit of the Spirit." All I remember about it is some woman teaching us a Jewish dance and people eating fruit with chocolate fondue as an analogy to the fruit of the Spirit. It just seemed like an excuse to get together and eat fruit and chocolate fondue with a little dance involved. We claimed the fruit of the Spirit was our theme, but it didn't have much to do with what we did.

As such a visual concept immortalized in beautiful pictures and Bible covers, the fruit of the Spirit has always intrigued me. I drafted sermon notes on the fruit of the Spirit many years back, (somewhere around 20 or so if I recall correctly) because I wanted to learn more about it. I was a younger minister then, still trying to figure out my calling in a maze of pastors and evangelists (not an apostle in sight), often confused and frustrated by what I saw. I was also considered very young by most standards. I can't say I understood everything about it back then, but I made my best effort to study what all these different things were that we called the "fruit of the Spirit."

At the time, let's just say I had a lot of issues. I was nowhere near close to displaying the fruit of the Spirit in my life, or even understanding it in any sort of semblance where my life could change because of it. I struggled through the study, looking up words and attempting to teach on the fruit of the Spirit to my almost non-existent congregation during the hot upstate New York summer months when fruit was in season.

Even though I had my issues and I could clearly see I had some work to do, I fell in love with the fruit of the Spirit. I didn't understand everything about it, but I knew it was important. I was surrounded by churches and leaders who made the fruit of the Spirit about materialism, and I really was not sure what God wanted to teach me – let alone teach anyone else – about this "fruit."

It would be many more years before I finally figured out just what God wanted to teach me and have me teach on the fruit of the Spirit. The fruit of the Spirit is not some nice, vague way to design a keychain. It's not an excuse to, once again, insert materialism into church teaching. What the fruit of the Spirit is, and should be to each one of us, is a gauge to identify where we are in the Spirit and where we are in our walk with God.

A really, really good fruit

To understand more about the fruit of the Spirit, let's start by looking at Galatians 5:22-23:

But the fruit of the Spirit is love, joy, peace, forbearance, kindness, goodness, faithfulness, gentleness and self-control. Against such things there is no law.

> **BUD BREAKS: Fruit**
> #2950 *karpos* [kar-pos']: fruit; that which originates or comes from something, an effect, result.

The Bible tells us clearly that there is a fruit, or product, from having the Spirit of God living and working inside of us. This is different from the spiritual gifts and signs and wonders we also receive from having the Spirit of God living and working within us (1 Corinthians 3:16, 2 Timothy 1:14). Those things prove that the

Spirit of God is alive and well, still doing wonders and impacting lives, even today. This book is not about the spiritual gifts that exist, although those are important to study if you are a believer (if you are interested to learn more about spiritual gifts, check out my book, *Manifestations of the Spirit: The Work of the Holy Spirit in the Church and in Your Life*). The reason I am not going to cover those in this book is because the past eight to ten years, there is so much out there on gifts, we are almost over-emphasizing them in a way that is out of balance and unhealthy to our spiritual health. Having gifts is great and awesome, and there is no doubt that spiritual gifts come from God. But we don't have spiritual gifts to make us feel good about ourselves, puff up our self-esteem, or so people will pay attention to us in a self-glorifying way. I believe so much teaching about being gifted has led people to ignore the principle of spiritual fruit, which we need alongside teaching about spiritual gifts. While gifts exist to build up the Body of Christ and ensure that every need is met, spiritual fruit is a product of the Spirit working within us, day in and day out, in a way that transforms and changes our outlook and our interactions with other people.

Live by the Spirit

It's great to study the fruit of the Spirit, but many people start studying Galatians chapter 5 in verse 22. If we are going to properly understand the fruit of the Spirit in an entire context, we need to start with verse 16. Verses 1-15 in Galatians 5 are about freedom in Christ and about the freedom we now have under God's grace. Beginning in verse 16 and going to verse 21, the Apostle Paul starts discussing the balance of freedom in grace, and that is life in the Spirit:

So I say, walk by the Spirit, and you will not gratify the desires of the flesh. For the flesh desires what is contrary to the Spirit, and the Spirit what is contrary to the flesh. They are in conflict with each other, so that you do not do whatever you want. But if you are led by the Spirit, you are not under law.

The acts of the sinful nature are obvious: sexual immorality, impurity and debauchery; idolatry and witchcraft; hatred, discord, jealousy, fits of rage, selfish ambition, dissentions, factions and envy; drunkenness, orgies and the like. I warn you, as I did before, that those who live like this will not inherit the Kingdom of God.

What we first need to understand about spiritual fruit is that the Apostle Paul made clear contrast between acceptable and unacceptable behaviors in Galatians 5. If we understand the statements made, it sounds like the church at Galatia had an awful lot of the same debates we see in church now. Rather than finding a balance between freedom and obedience, grace and principle, people swung from one extreme to the other. Having lived under various laws (whether Jewish or pagan), the people of Galatia understood legalism, but did not understand grace. Some believed grace and freedom to mean anyone could do anything they wanted, while others stood on the sidelines and argued that people needed the law. The Apostle Paul's clarity was to prove that if we are truly living in God's freedom and under His grace, we will walk in the Spirit and display the fruit of the Spirit. If we are truly following the Spirit, then certain things will display that change. In other words: if we are in the Spirit, it will show.

> **POWER POLLINATION:** When dealing with others (especially non-believers) avoid the temptation to label people in one way or another, especially to call attention to the fact that "they're sinners." The Bible says that all have sinned and fallen short of the glory of God (Romans 3:23). It's fine to discuss sin, but labeling people in such a manner exhibits judgment, because your sins are just as bad in the eyes of God as theirs are.

The Apostle Paul begins by explaining to us that we are to live by the Spirit, and that means not gratifying the flesh. Ugh…the part everyone hates. Whether we want to hear about it or not, there are things that every fiber of our being wants to do…and those things are not of God. We want to scream in the face of someone who was rude to us, or we want to hop into bed with the cute guy or girl we met on the subway, or we just want to throw that tantrum because we didn't get our way, or we want to envy the person who got "promoted" when we got passed up, or we want to gossip about pastor or apostle when they didn't give us our way…or…or…or…

The list goes on and on. Every one of us is a sinner and every one of us has displayed actions that displayed that sinful nature. Looking at the Apostle Paul's evidence there of the sinful nature should humble us and make us realize how much farther we all need to go and how much better we all can do if we will let the Spirit take over in our lives. See, the purpose and point of the law was to make us aware that we are sinners, not able to do right by our own means and attempts (Galatians 3:24, Galatians 4:1-31). The purpose of the law is to bring out all the sinful natures on that list and call to attention that, no matter how good we try to do this thing on our own, we are not going to be successful.

> **BUD BREAKS: Spirit** #4151 *pneuma* [pnyoo'-mah]: 1) a movement of air (a gentle blast); the spirit, i.e. the vital principal by which the body is animated; 3) a spirit, i.e. a simple essence, devoid of all or at least all grosser matter, and possessed of the power of knowing, desiring, deciding, and acting; 4) of God; 5) the disposition or influence which fills and governs the soul of any one.

The good news: if you are led by the Spirit, you are not under the law! Who-hoo! We all see that verse and cheer real loud…but wait! It says if you are led by the Spirit. In other words: it is about more than just being Spirit-filled, or believing in the Spirit! It is about being so full of the Spirit, you allow the Spirit to come into your life and lead all your steps and actions. If you are truly led by the Spirit, you are not under the law, because you have no need for being under the law…because you won't violate it.

It's important to see that, as we study the fruit of the Spirit, we recognize the fruit of the Spirit is not based on emotions or emotional states. There is nothing wrong with having feelings! Not every feeling we have in our lives is going to be upbeat or positive. There will be plenty of days when we have feelings that people deem as being "negative," whether they are anger, sadness, or grief. These feelings are not, in and of themselves, sinful. The Bible never tells us that anger, sadness, grief, or feeling a little "down" are considered sins. The Bible tells us not to act rashly in our emotional states (Ephesians 4:26), and it does caution us against being led by these emotions, because it is possible to act sinfully if we let our emotions get the best of us (Psalm 4:4). There are things that should make us feel angry, or things that should make us feel sad, or down, all within the normal course of life. These are often reactions to other people's sins or sinful states, and it would be abnormal if we responded to all of them with a smile. We can have feelings; those feelings do not indicate that the Spirit cannot or is not at work within us. What clearly defines we are not being led by the Spirit are actions. These actions are:

- **Sexual immorality**: Sexuality is a necessary physical drive most people have, so the human species might continue. In a bigger sense, it's a way that many people desire to connect in various physically intimate ways throughout their lifetimes. It's not the only way we connect, nor is it the most important, but it is still, nonetheless, a valid way to connect. The thing we need to consider about sexuality is that it is a very, very strong drive that, when improperly fueled and fed, can take on a life of its own. I am not going to go over the very long list of sexual "isms" that people argue over, but I think we can boil sexual immorality down to crossing lines of personal integrity, respect, and dignity. Whenever sex or sexual interaction is clearly lacking these elements, it is clearly a case where sexual immorality is present.

- **Impurity**: The Bible talks a lot about purity (Psalm 119:9, Matthew 5:8, 1 Timothy 4:12). Many believe the command of purity to be merely sexual, but it is not. To be pure means to lack sin in thought, word, and action. It is a state of being untouched by sin in one's personal life. To be impure means to be the opposite; It is to be consumed by sin and sinful actions.

- **Debauchery**: Debauchery is an older term that indicates one indulges in everything they find pleasing to their senses.

It represents a lifestyle of over-indulgence and gluttony.

- **Idolatry**: Idolatry is when an individual puts anything in the place of God in their lives. We often assume an idolater is someone bowing before a golden calf somewhere or worshipping a pagan god. It is not incorrect to attribute such behaviors to idolatry, but it is wrong to assume that's where idolatry starts and ends. Idolatry can take any form…can affect any person of any theological understanding…and can run a spectrum of forms. If it's between you and God or someone else and God, it doesn't matter what it is…it's an idol.

- **Witchcraft**: When we think of witchcraft, most of us think of a circle of witches around a big, black pot, chanting spells and stealing the warts off toads. This is a cartoonish-style image that Hollywood has given us about witches and what witchcraft is. Most witches you, as a Christian, will meet, don't wear a black pointy hat. They don't carry around a broomstick and they don't cackle

> **FOUNDATIONAL FERTILIZER:** When I was a teenager, a faction emerged within the Catholic parish I attended. The group advocated a reversion to the "old ways" of Catholicism, doing things the way they were done in the church before the Second Vatican Council. When they did not get their way, they began taking out ads in the newspaper, coming against the local pastor and the administrative staff, even handing out literature and cards after weekend masses! They were quick to spread their stories anywhere and everywhere anyone would listen. At first, everyone was very concerned that they would destroy the parish. As time went on, however, their voices were dulled, and no one was as interested in what they had to say. Why? They became a lot of noise. Factions seem larger than life at the time, but they always die out if they are allowed to follow their own course and self-destruct.

over a pot. Witchcraft, simply put, is control. It is when an individual seeks to exert their will over someone else's, with no regard for what that individual may want or desire. Someone might appear to be praying (when it is really spell-casting), to be very interested in someone, to be talking about people a lot, or to just be very controlling, dominating people. However you spin it…it's witchcraft.

- **Hatred**: Hatred is the condition of hating someone. It's more than not having a high regard for someone, because any one of us can disregard someone because of their attitude or behavior. It is defined in many ways, but includes prejudice, hostility, or animosity. It is an unwarranted, unexplainable disdain for someone else, that comes from an intense inner virulence toward another person or group.

- **Discord**: Discord is the state of bringing about deliberate disagreement to clash. It is intending to be deliberately difficult and to deliberately bring disharmony and disunity to a situation, without warrant. I think we can all think of lots of people who amplify the state of discord in life, especially on the internet, on social media networks, and especially in church.

- **Jealousy**: To be jealous is to be at rivalry with others because of what one perceives they have or are doing, with or without warrant for such conduct. For example, someone who is jealous in a relationship is overly suspicious and judgmental of the actions of that other person, even if there is no call for such behavior. (For the sake of clarity, let's say now: jealousy is not a compliment, nor is it flattering; rather, it's a sin. It can also become dangerous.) Akin to jealousy is covetousness, or desiring to own or hold on to someone or something beyond a boundary that is normal and healthy.

- **Fits of rage**: We might call this a "temper tantrum" to make it sound cute, but fits of rage in any form: explosive tempers, picking fights, abusing other people physically, verbally, emotionally or sexually, throwing fits, behaving badly, or otherwise acting in ways that are unseemly are not in alignment with godly conduct. It is fine to be angry, it is not fine to take your anger out on everyone else.

- **Selfish ambition**: Ambition in and of itself is not a bad thing. It's great to aspire to be a great leader, or a great Christian, or great at your job. The problem is when ambition becomes all about pleasing yourself, no matter who or what gets hurt in the crossfire. If your ambitions are only to benefit you and ignore the welfare of everyone else around you, that is a selfish ambition.

> **PRUNING POINTS:** We all can think of obvious examples of sinful behavior from before we were saved, but keep in mind that the Apostle Paul lists many sinful actions here that may not be seen with the naked eye. Envy, selfish ambition, jealousy and hatred are not things that are always easily seen unless one looks with a discerning eye or one behaves in an obviously overt way. How can you grow out of some of the "not so obvious" areas of sin – and move more toward the fruit of the Spirit?

- **Dissentions**: Dissention disagrees to the point of arguing in a contentious and blindly biased manner. This means that someone who argues just to argue a point even in the face of clear evidence to the contrary is becoming dissentious. It is being argumentative without objectivity, especially in the face of realizing the truth is everything but what someone is saying.

- **Factions**: A faction forms as a small group existing within a larger group that takes its position against the beliefs and standings of the larger group. They are motivated by an attention-seeking spirit and seek to cause trouble. For example, if someone is in a church and they believe the pastor is not really doing anything morally wrong, but not doing things the way the faction likes, they may start talking to other people in the hopes and advocacy that the pastor will be pressured to change. Factions are a form of passive-aggressive behavior that encourages disunity and miscommunication within a group.

- **Envy**: Envy is a step up from jealousy in that it's a more intense form of it. When one is envious, it is obvious that they are lacking the thing that they see in someone else or that someone else has, and it reaches a point where they desire to possess it so it consumes their life. Envy isn't always obvious, where someone stalks someone else or tries to take away their job or opportunities. Sometimes envy manifests in the desire to outdo someone else or be better than them, with jealousy as an underlying factor.

- **Drunkenness**: To be drunk is to be intoxicated, indicating someone has had more alcohol to drink than their body can handle. The Bible speaks extensively on the sin of drunkenness (Proverbs 20:1, Proverbs 23:20-35, Isaiah 5:11, Isaiah 5:22, Isaiah 28:7, 1 Corinthians 5:11, Ephesians 5:18). We can also apply the principle of intoxication to extend to any drug, illegal or legal, used for the purpose of escapism, intoxication, or a "high."

- **Orgies**: We've come to associate an orgy with group sexual activity or group sex, but this isn't how the ancients described an orgy. In ancient cultures, orgies were pagan religious rituals open only to certain people who operated with a certain level of authority in each religious group. They were a part of ancient understandings of witchcraft in connection with sexual fertility rites, by which the participants engaged in sexual activity with one another or with certain people in the group to unite with the divine. Rather than just being a frenzied attempt to have sex with as many people as possible, an orgy was understood to be a mystical rite. The reason it was prohibited is because it was intimately connected to witchcraft and with uniting oneself to false, demonic gods and goddesses.

- **The "like"**: Indicates things like those listed above, whether in action or appearance.

The list above covers just about anything we can conceive of when it comes to obvious sinful natures. While doing these things might please us in the flesh or bring us gratification temporarily, they are a clear sign that we are not allowing ourselves to follow the nature of the Spirit. We should carefully heed the Apostle Paul's words that if we are engaging in the acts of sinful nature, we won't inherit the Kingdom of God. Part of being in God's Kingdom is submitting to His Spirit. If we are not attentive to the Spirit as Spirit-led people, we will not be able to follow God's leadings in our lives.

Against these things there is no law

The Apostle Paul ends verse 23 by saying:

Against such things there is no law.

> **BUD BREAKS: Law**
> #3551 *nomos* [nom'-os]: anything established, anything received by usage, a custom, a law, a command.

Any one of us could go anywhere in the world and find laws that prohibit the sinful behaviors listed above. In fact, we can probably find many laws in many different countries with respect to the things listed above in many different contexts. In contrast to the list of sinful behaviors above, the fruit of the Spirit is none of these things and looks nothing like these things. The fruit of the Spirit manifests as love, joy, peace, patience, kindness, goodness, faithfulness, gentleness, and self-control. While there might be laws against all the sinful things listed, there is no law against manifesting the fruit of the Spirit. Nowhere in the world does any government prohibit displaying the fruit of the Spirit in one's life. This means that if we are truly walking in the Spirit, we will not violate any law, either legal or spiritual, anywhere we go. Verses 24-26 go on to say:

Those who belong to Christ Jesus have crucified the flesh with its passions and desires. Since we live by the Spirit, let us keep in step with the Spirit. Let us not become conceited, provoking and envying each other.

It's important to keep in mind that the Apostle Paul's words were written to the church, not to the world. It's easy to read the list of sinful behaviors and automatically tick off lists of people we know in our heads who display those sorts of behaviors. This means that we, as the church, should always be doing self-examination when we hear these words spoken and when we read them ourselves, not just thinking about everyone else who should apply them. We are called to keep in step with the Spirit, because the Spirit is alive and active (Romans 8:26-27, Ephesians 4:30, 1 John 5:7-8). The Spirit will guide us into all truth, in every situation we step into, and will not lead us into sin, regardless of the situation at hand. Don't fall behind the Spiri, or ahead of the Spirit, and certainly don't come into a place where you are provoking or envying others, because that will lead you to fall out of step with the Spirit and back into sin.

> **HAPPY HARVEST:** Even though this book is not specifically about spiritual gifts, do you walk in your spiritual gifts, and understand their role in your life? To learn more about the gifts given to everyone in the church as God wills, read 1 Corinthians 12:4-11 and Romans 12:4-8. Where do you fit in the church, to build it up and edify it?

Today we hear a lot about faith and having faith, but we don't hear a lot about what to do with that faith. I've met plenty of people who might have enough faith to get into heaven, but they don't have enough faith to impact the lives of people around them. The fruit that we are walking in our faith unto a victory and overcoming the sinful nature of our lives is the fruit of the Spirit, harming none, seeking to offend none, and doing no wrong to

God, our fellow brethren in Christ, our neighbor, or ourselves.

Obviously, we all have a long way to go, but don't be discouraged. If it's the first time you're considering these issues in your lives, it's all right. No matter how long you've been a believer, we can all benefit from good lessons on the fruit of the Spirit and applying them for ourselves. None of us are perfect, and all of us can use refreshers as well as encouragements to examine ourselves so we can do better as we walk through our spiritual lives.

One, unified fruit

The first thing I remember noticing when it came to the fruit of the Spirit is that nine different things are mentioned in connection with the Spirit, but it isn't spoken of in a plurality. The fruit of the Spirit is not spoken of as "fruits," but as one singular fruit. Even though a cluster of grapes is made up of many berries, it is still spoken of as one cluster, and the cluster is described as the "fruit of the vine." An orange is made up of many membrane sections, but it is still only one fruit. The reason the fruit of the Spirit is spoken of in the same terms is because the fruit of the Spirit is one fruit! It takes all nine components to make up one fruit. You might have part of the fruit, you might have none of the fruit, or you might have all the fruit, but it is still one unified piece of fruit, one unified manifestation of the Spirit in one's life. Just as there is only one Spirit (1 Corinthians 12:4, 11) and many gifts, there is only one fruit of the Spirit, with different ways that fruit manifests in one's life. The unity of the fruit of the Spirit reminds us that our end goal is to be more united to God, and to those who are truly of His Kingdom.

If you are in Christ, you can walk in the Spirit

The good news about the fruit of the Spirit is that it's not impossible to walk in it. If you are truly in Christ, then you can walk away from sinful things, handle temptations as they come along, and grow as a believer. Don't worry, we will talk about all these issues in this book, one at a time, so that it is easy to understand.

Are you ready to walk in the Spirit with evidence of fruit? There's a vine and many branches waiting and ready to welcome you.

Chapter Two

Love

Place me like a seal over your heart,
like a seal on your arm;
for love is as strong as death,
its jealousy unyielding as the grave.
It burns like blazing fire, like a mighty flame.
Many waters cannot quench love;
rivers cannot sweep it away.
If one were to give all the wealth of one's house for love,
it would be utterly scorned.
– Song of Solomon 8:6-7

Assignments:
- Read 1 Corinthians 13:1-13.
- Reach out in some way to someone that you cared about, but have lost contact with.
- Take on a church or community service project that reaches out to others in love.

Society tells us if we love other people, we won't ever disagree with them about anything. If we love them, we will let them do whatever they want, never tell them no, and never in any way offer a counterpoint to their lives. The church often poses a complete extreme to this viewpoint. Many in church feel that we show people love by being disagreeable and argumentative with them in the name of one of three things: "Christian love," "holiness," and "truth." We think if we don't voice our nastily stated opinions on every topic, we aren't showing others an accurate picture of spiritual truth.

For many years, I fell into both extremes. Watching people act the way they did made me think maybe the key to love was not disagreeing with others and never offering counterpoint to their lives. I went from this extreme to the complete opposite, voicing every thought I had in a bossy, demanding manner. I believed I could argue others into the Kingdom with words and smart-sounding arguments. The only problem was that people would come back with their own arguments (that I never thought were good enough). All we would do was argue back and forth. It was, in reality, the opposite of love. It took a sobering look at myself and a lot of study and reflection to start finding balance on the topic of love. It's often something we don't easily understand, nor do we live to the fullest. I will admit, I am still learning when it comes to loving others. The answer to love is somewhere in the middle between complete permissiveness and intolerant hostility: something else, something that seeks the very best for others in each and every possible situation.

> **PRUNING POINTS:** In discussing the ways we substitute the word "love" for "like," what are some things you describe as "loving," but you really like a lot? How can rewording your terminology help you to gain a better understanding of what love is in your life?

Love is a topic that makes many people uncomfortable. I believe this is because we overuse the term "love" and use it with many different connotations today. As a result, we really don't understand what it is anymore. We don't distinguish love from like. We think love is a cute notion for a wedding or a romantic interlude, many equate love with sex, and then there are the myriad of other things we say we love in a day: social media, reality TV, shoes, dessert, hot K-pop stars, vacation time, and beyond. We've come to equate love with sex, love with shopping, and love with everything except what really is love and what we should really be defining as love. Then we try to have our moments where we come into church and say we love God, or we love our neighbor, or we love our spouse, or significant other, or friends, or whoever it is we want to tell them we love them…and we throw the term "love" in there when we are actually intending to be condescending or insulting, or make someone else feel small, and us great.

None of the things I've said thus far should sound like love, but an awful lot of people in the world equate love with these different things. It shouldn't be a wonder that people don't respond well when we try to tell them that God loves them, because they can't equate the love of God with the things they've experienced and the things people stand and tell them. This means if we are going to start this off right, we need to do it the right way, and really understand just what love is and how love can change the world in the way God desires it to.

What is love?

Before we all break into Haddaway's hit song from the 90s that asks that question, I think answering "What is love?" is like trying to answer, "What is air?" We know it's there, we know we need it, we know it's essential to life, but in the long run…what is it, really? For thousands of years, people have tried to sing about it, people have tried to write about it in poems, people have tried to figure it out, seek it out, and discover it for themselves, but nobody seems to be able to explain it in a way that seems to clarify for us exactly what it is. It has not helped that people associate it with different things and many times the things they associate it with aren't love and don't point us to love. 1 John 4:7-12 tells us:

Dear friends, let us love one another, for love comes from God. Everyone who loves has been born of God and knows God. Whoever does not love does not know God, because God is love. This is how God showed His love among us: He sent His one and only Son into the world that we might live through Him. This is love: not that we loved God, but that He loved us and sent His Son as an atoning sacrifice for our sins. Dear friends, since God so loved us, we also ought to love one another. No one has ever seen God; but if we love one another, God lives in us and His love is made complete in us.

The simplest answer to what love is, is to say that God is love. God is love because He not only entrusted us with His entire world, He also gave to us through the sacrifice of Christ. God so desired that we would have relationship with Him, He was willing to even give us His Son. This tells us some essential things about love:

- **Love gives of itself**: We can't say we love if it doesn't cost us something.

- **Love gains something**: As God gave of His Son, He also restored our relationship and connection with Him.

- **Love completes**: The longing of the ages is fulfilled in Christ. There is a fulfilled completion in love, something that closes one door, and opens another unto eternity.

- **Love is seen in us**: Even though we can't see God, if we have love within us, people can know God exists and that He is real.

Some people argue love is an emotion, but this is not entirely correct. When people compare love to an emotion, they are tying infatuation and attraction to it. Others argue love is an action. While I can't deny that love does have action attached to it, people can do things all day long with no love behind them. This is why love, in and of itself, is both motivated by something that God places within us that forces us to express it in some form.

> **BUD BREAKS: Love**
> #26 *agape* {ag-ah'-pay}:
> 1) brotherly love, affection, good will, love; benevolence
> 2) love feasts.

I teach that love is an underlying principle. If love is understood to be an underlying principle, running as a thread through all things, then it has the power to transform and transcend thought, word, and deed. This is the kind of love God desires us to have; a love that transforms and runs through every aspect of our lives. If love is only a decision, it can transform thought, but not word or action. If it is only an emotion, it can change our words and deeds, but only at whim, as we feel like changing them. If it is in doing, then it does not transform our thoughts or our words. Love must transcend to transform, and that means love is a principle. It is something we believe by, think by, speak by, do by, and ultimately, live by.

Types of love in the Bible

In the first edition of this book, I spoke of the four classical Greek words for love, having been taught they were Biblical words. I have since learned that while some of them are in the Bible and their principles are definitely Biblical, there are actually other words for "love" in Scripture. Most of them are parallel to one another. The basic terms for "love" as surround Scripture are: *'Ahab* and *eros*, *raham* and *phileo*, *hesed*, *storgay*, and *agape*.

- **'Ahab and Eros**: Although not exactly the same, ahab and eros can be rough equivalents of one another in root understanding. *'Ahab*, as the first term used in the Hebrew Old Testament to describe love, is a "catch-all" term. Its concepts include sexual attraction and love, love between people, friendship, human interests, appetite, desire, lovers, God's love toward humanity, something lovely, and like. *Eros* is a little more simplistic and used in the Septuagint (the Greek translation of the Old Testament), especially in the Song of Solomon. It is used to describe sexual attraction, desire, interest, or that sexual interest in connection. The word is always used in the sense of attraction and seeks gratification and pleasure in that context. It's how a man or a woman can say, "I love my spouse, but I am not in love with them." They are saying that even though they might love them as a person, they are not attracted to them anymore.

For the sake of our understanding, I would say both *'ahab* and *eros* can be translated as both desire and attraction. In love, we are drawn to something, and both these words express the simplistic idea that when we love, we are drawn by something in form.

- **Raham/phileo**: Both *raham* (Hebrew) and *phileo* (Greek) describe characteristics of friendship. Under these subheadings, we find the idea of love, deep love, mercy, compassion, tender affection, brotherly love, love between siblings, and love among the church. They describe something more than just a mere casual acquaintance, but it's not sexual or romantic in nature. We could define it as a loving friendship, one based on a bond where a friend is "closer than a brother" (Proverbs 18:24).

- **Storgay (philostorgos)**: A Greek word that defines a love for one's relatives, especially in the context of a familial bond. We could define this term as "familial honor" or "familial alliance."

- **Hesed**: A Hebrew word often translated in one of four ways: goodness, kindness, faithfulness, or most infamously, as lovingkindness. As a form of spiritual drawing, it is something we both feel (God places it within us), and then pushes us to do something with it. By acting through *hesed*, we exemplify certain aspects of God's character within ourselves, showing love rather than just claiming it.

- **Agape**: *Agape*, a Greek term, is considered the highest, or most intense, form of love. Whenever the Bible speaks of loving God, loving our neighbor, or displaying the love of God to one another, it always speaks of *agape*. It is divine love, completely spiritual in nature, that seeks the greatest good for everyone involved. It is associated with unselfishness. In Galatians 5:22, the "love" spoken of in connection with the fruit of the Spirit is *agape* and is what we will be talking about here in this book.

> **HAPPY HARVEST:** How can you invite the Spirit to live in you in a more profound way? We know the Spirit abides best where He is welcome, so how can you make the Spirit feel more at home within you?

It's obvious there are many different forms of human interaction that we define as "love." Because love is based on relationship, there are different ways love is understood. Using the term "love," therefore, is complicated. It's not easy to understand or to define, because it is based on how we understand it. Most, if not all people, will walk in most forms of love at some point in their lives, both giving and receiving them. *Agape*, however, is a different matter. As the highest form of love, it should be at the root of all of our relationships, the foundation of our interactions with others, and the very thing that transforms out relationship with God.

The foundation to our spiritual house

In thinking of the fruit of the Spirit, I think of it as building a house. The fruit of the Spirit can be parallel to our spiritual house, the place where we allow the Spirit to dwell within us and transform our entire lives. Love is the foundation of that house. When a house is built, the foundation is the most essential aspect of building that house. Even though it might not be pretty, the foundation holds up the entire structure and keeps it from sinking into the ground. If the foundation cracks or wears away, the entire building will either fall or seriously deteriorate, and it becomes very expensive to repair.

If love is the foundation for our spiritual house, it's important we have a good foundation of it in our lives. Love is the fruit of the Spirit! If we don't have love, we won't have the rest of the attributes and won't be able to display the fruit of the Spirit in any other way.

The two most important commandments

The New Testament drives home the importance of love, many times over. Perhaps the most important word on love is found in Mark 12:28-34:

One of the teachers of the law came and heard them debating. Noticing that Jesus had given them a good answer, he asked Him, "Of all the commandments, which is the most important?"

"The most important one," answered Jesus, "is this: 'Hear, O Israel, the Lord our God, the Lord is one. Love the Lord your God with all your heart and with all your soul and with all your mind and with all your strength.' The second is this: 'Love your neighbor as yourself.' There is no commandment greater than these."

"Well said, teacher," the man replied. "You are right in saying that God is one and there is no other but Him. To love Him with all your heart, with all your understanding and with all your strength, and to love your neighbor as yourself is more important than all burnt offerings and sacrifices."

When Jesus saw that he had answered wisely, He said to him, "You are not far from the Kingdom of God." And from then on no one dared ask Him any more questions.

Love is so vital and so important; it hinges on the most important of all imaginable commandments. It is the height of all we seek, desire, and ascribe to be. We are to love God above all and love our neighbor as ourselves. That sounds easy enough, right?

It's obvious from the passage above that loving God and loving one's neighbor sounds "easy enough" on paper. One can read the Bible, as the scribes and Pharisees of old did, and see what God asks of us in theory. We can talk about loving God and loving one another all day long, but living it is another thing all together. It'll be easy after Jesus comes back and everyone is on the same page. This side of heaven, loving God means we honor Him and do what He asks of us. That gets tricky the second we want to do something different from God's will for us. It's easy to love our neighbor in theory when they leave us alone and don't do anything we don't like, but it gets tricky when we must love our difficult, nasty, contrary neighbor…or our neighbor who doesn't look like us…or act like us…or believe like us…or isn't…us.

When Jesus spoke of these commandments, He spoke of the principle I mentioned earlier. Love needs to become so much a part of us that it flows through us, flowing through from our relationship with God to other people. Since God is love and He lives in us (1 John 4:12), we must step aside from our proclivities to sin and allow the Spirit to move through us so we can let love become a powerful part of us.

Attributes of love

We love hearing 1 Corinthians 13:1-13 at weddings because it sounds all sweet and poetic. When was the last time we stopped and considered what it is trying to tell us? 1 Corinthians 13 is not talking about familial love, or sexual love, or friendship, but it is talking about *agape* love. It wasn't just written to be a nice, cute thing to put on a plaque and send to all your friends when they get married. 1 Corinthians 13 demands that we all step back and consider the excellence God demands of us in love and how we can identify *agape* love versus other things people call "love."

1 Corinthians 13:1-3:

If I speak in the tongues of men or of angels, but do not have love, I am only a resounding gong or a clanging cymbal. If I have the gift of prophecy and can fathom all mysteries and all knowledge, and if I have a faith that can move mountains, but do not have love, I am nothing. If I give all I possess to the poor and give over my body to hardship that I may boast, but do not have love, I gain nothing.

God knew the term "love" would be all-too-casually used. 1 Corinthians 13 proves that people in church have always been casual about big displays of their faith, relying too much on spiritual gifts to prove something they were never intended to prove. We can do all the church things we think we are supposed to do in the traditional church manner. We can scream at the devil when our lights get turned off because we didn't pay the bill, we can be the loudest tongue talker in the church, we can read a million books and spout off our extensive knowledge of all things doctrinal, we can be the first one in line to make the biggest contribution to the soup kitchen…but if we don't have love…none of it matters, nor is any of it worth anything.

1 Corinthians 13:4-7:

Love is patient, love is kind. It does not envy, it does not boast, it is not proud. It does not dishonor others, it is not self-seeking, it is not easily angered, it keeps no record of wrongs. Love does not delight in evil but rejoices with the truth. It always protects, always trusts, always hopes, always perseveres.

These three verses of 1 Corinthians 13 prove that love is the essence of the fruit of the Spirit. Joy, peace, patience, kindness, goodness, faithfulness, gentleness, and self-control are all attributes mentioned here, some worded in the same way, and some worded in other ways. It outright tells us that love is patient (long-suffering, faithful), kind (reflecting kindness), not envious (joyful), does not boast (good), is not proud (peaceful), not easily angered (patient, self-controlled), and keeps no record of wrong (kind, good, joyful). It is the opposite of everything we want to do for our own selfish motives and purposes. Simply put, love considers others and wants to do right not just by self, but by others. Love protects, trusts, hopes, and perseveres. It always makes the effort, and always does what is right.

1 Corinthians 13:8-12:

Love never fails. But where there are prophecies, they will cease; where there are tongues, they will be stilled; where there is knowledge, it will pass away. For we know in part and we prophecy in part, but when completeness comes, what is in part disappears. When I was a child, I talked like a child, I thouthg like a child, I reasoned like a child. When I became a man, I put the ways of childhood behind me. For now we see only a reflection as in a mirror; then we shall see face to face. Now I know in part; then I shall know fully, even as I am fully known.

The Apostle Paul was not trying to create a new doctrine in this passage. He wasn't arguing for the cessation of spiritual gifts or that they would cease before Jesus comes back. 1 Corinthians 14 proves this to the letter, because it is an entire discourse on using spiritual gifts in an orderly and disciplined fashion in worship settings. If anything, He was saying those things would exist until completeness (Jesus) reappears in the Second Coming (after that, they won't be needed anymore). What the Apostle was trying to tell us is that as of right now, we are people, still in fleshly bodies. We do not know or assess everything perfectly. We don't have perfect insight, and sometimes, no matter how spiritual we may feel at that moment, don't get it all right. We are only seeing part of the picture this side of heaven. If we over-emphasize certain aspects of faith and take them to a place that is out of balance or without consideration for the virtues and attributes we are to develop, we won't have a complete picture of our faith. To talk incessantly about spiritual gifts and ignore teaching on love or on ways to live in love completely misses the point of our faith and living our faith.

1 Corinthians 13:13:

And now these three remain: faith, hope, and love. But the greatest of these is love.

Love is the greatest because it is God, Who represents every attribute of love imaginable. Faith is great, and what we do for faith is great. It is eternal. Hope is great, and having hope, living in hope, and dwelling in hope is an extension of our life of faith. The greatest, however, is love…because God Himself is love. If we are in Him, we can dwell in love with Him forever.

Loving God and each other

We could talk all day long about loving God and our neighbor. What it means to love God is something that almost can't be expressed in mere words. In accepting Who God is: the fullness of His role as our Creator, Redeemer, Sustainer, Provider, and Healer, it makes us want to extend toward Him what we have received from Him…that is, our very lives. He has given us life, so it makes us want to offer our lives unto Him. By doing such, we make a statement of clear and defined trust in Him. We are proving we take Him at His Word and that His Word is not only good for us, but also enough. We know and trust that as we walk with Him, He will lead us into every good place. We praise Him, we pray to Him and share with Him, we worship Him, because we love Who He is as we grow and learn more about Him in our lives.

This doesn't mean we understand everything about our relationship with God all the time. Just as the Apostle Paul pointed out in 1 Corinthians 13 that we know in part, we know God in part, as well. We don't always understand why He asks us to do what He asks of us, nor do we always want to do it. Obedience is sometimes difficult. Trust is sometimes difficult. As with other relationships in our lives, we might find ourselves

> **FOUNDATIONAL FERTILIZER:** I've often told people that I strongly dislike presiding at weddings, because I feel they are a big, gigantic show that doesn't prepare people for the realities of marriage. In focusing so much on fancy parties, venues, and expensive clothing, brides and grooms are missing something in their experiences. It's more important that pre-wedding couples learn the principles of *agape* and consideration for one another than they learn how to do anything else in their marriage.

sometimes upset…but in love, we stand up and do what is asked of us. We trust…We praise…We worship through our trials and our difficulties, knowing our Father in heaven loves us and will take care of us, right to the end.

There are probably thousands of books in existence that attempt to define the relationship between God and those who love Him. Loving our neighbor is the thing that we haven't written volumes on, because we are still trying to figure it out. Yet if we don't understand it, that probably explains why we don't understand the proper way to evangelize the world. We live in a hurting world that is marred by doctrinal concepts of various spiritual laws and confused about what God's love can offer them. When we love our neighbor, that means we seek the best for them, even if they – or we – can't see what that is right now.

Paralleling 1 Corinthians 13, we can best explain how to show our neighbor we love them: display a sincere and genuine interest in who they are as people. Too often we are a little too eager to play "Holy Ghost, Jr." and try to "'fix" what we deem wrong with someone else. We're too quick to tell others they are "going to hell" or "God is not pleased" because of something we perceive. Let's never forget that nowhere in the New Testament did anyone go forth and proclaim hell to people who did not know the Lord. They went and brought good news, telling people that the Kingdom of Heaven was near, as close as anyone could reach out and touch. So…is it at all possible that the manner in which we reach out needs a change?

"Holiness or hell" preaching might be popular among those who long for the familiarity of older times, but it's doing nothing to change the world and bring it to the Lord. Fire and brimstone have never worked. What has always worked is a right heart, a right motive, and a right intent. We show people we love them by listening to them, concerning ourselves with the things that they are concerned about, by being kind and offering what we can to their plights and difficulties, by paying attention to their interests and supporting those that are leading them to a great place in their lives. Show that you care. Take someone to lunch, have coffee with them, encourage them as a person. Be a good friend to those you meet. Do something besides yell at others, shouting Bible verses in between.

Love in intimate connections

Most advice for dating couples, spouses, and individuals who are in some sort of intimate relationship (even in church circles) focuses a lot on the "rules" people have made for *eros* attachments and involvements. People are so afraid someone might have sex before they get married that we've made weddings the dividing point between pre-sex and post-sex acceptability. The advice for marriages, discussions for marriages, and thoughts for marriage are almost always around sex: what is acceptable, what is not acceptable, and what the couple should be doing at every stage of their marriage.

It's fine, even necessary, for couples to discuss their sexual relationship. Before that ever happens, however, couples should be considering the ways that *agape* should take hold of their lives and change their relationship. Most marital problems occur because one or both partners are not considering their partner in the way they should, thus causing one or both partners to feel slighted. *Eros* is not going to solve all the problems couples will have. Eventually that good-looking partner that "turns you on" is not going to make up for inconsiderate or rude behavior. Every single couple needs to have an *agape* root at the base of their marriage. Marital partners need to love each other as people before they ever love one another as lovers. This means that, while dating or courting, couples need to talk, they need to keep a check on their physical desires and not cross certain boundaries that can blur the lines of character in a potential mate, and it also means they need time and the distance away from the influences of friends and family members to see what they need to realize in the other person for themselves. Both parties need to understand the principle of mutual submission, whereby both individuals in the marriage recognize the gifts and abilities the other has and submit to the place where God wants to take those gifts and that individual in their lives (Ephesians 5:21-33). Couples need to understand that support is mutual, and both will have to make sacrifices and compromises throughout their marriage. Making those compromises shows the other person that

> **FOUNDATIONAL FERTILIZER:** When I was first born again and desired to be serious about my walk with God, that meant I was no longer able to be a part of my church of origin. When I was growing up, there was a woman in our parish who was just the "salt of the earth." She was always of service, considered extremely selfless, devoting her time to volunteering and helping out others. One of her major themes was "Christian unity," so I figured that, whether Catholic or not, she would be willing to help me get started in ministry. Imagine my shock and horror when every time she was asked to help, she refused! One day, while I was in prayer, God revealed to me that she didn't help me was because helping me back then would not get her a lot of acclaim. I wasn't big enough, nor important enough, for a big fuss to come from her help. God then reminded me if I was going to do His work, I couldn't be like her. When helping others, are you doing it to be noticed...or to genuinely help?

they are loved, and also opens the door for God to flow freely in between the partners. If a couple does not have *agape*, that couple will not survive as a couple.

On a side note: Love doesn't mean staying through abuse or mistreatment. Remember, *agape* goes both ways. It's even possible to be two people who love God individually, as people, but who are unable to come together and reflect the necessary love they must have to love God as a couple. If a relationship becomes abusive, over certain boundary lines, or in any way spirals to a place that is clearly out of control, the love of God does not demand you stay there. We are to love others as we love ourselves. That means because God is working through us, we have enough regard for what He has done and is doing within us to walk away from anything that compromises His image present within our very selves and lives.

Love in families

We talk about love in families in the limited context of *storgay* because that is a comfortable understanding for us. People assume that because individuals are in a family, that family should have that sense of "us vs. the world" within it. What we don't teach enough on in church is that love among a family needs to be more than identifying for the purposes of a family clan or family defense. We need *agape* in our families as much as we need it anywhere else, because *agape* establishes a forum of understanding.

Above all things people say they want in this life, people want to understand and belong. *Agape* opens the door for this among families, where people do not always like who they are "stuck" with thanks to biology. We can love people and not like them, because like is not a lesser form of love. God doesn't always like us or what we are doing, but He does always love us. In *agape*, we can begin to see why God commands us to do the things He does for our families throughout the Scriptures, and it's not out of a sense of familial clan or duty. The call to honor our father and mother (Exodus 20:12) is out of *agape*; it is respecting them as human beings, with their own life story, as people who gave part of their lives to help develop ours. Whether biological, adopted, or extended family caregivers, this concept shows appreciation for that. Respecting parents (Ephesians 6:1-3), parents loving children and not over-disciplining them (Ephesians 6:4), and showing love and respect to our extended family members raises people up as individuals, rather than just showing some sort of great force to overtake other families.

Love among friends

Agape love is easiest to show among our friends because we choose our friends. As a rule, our friends are selected for various qualities that we either like or that complement our own. Just as all relationships change, however, our friendships change, as well. Sometimes our lives change and our interests, friends, and desires toward our friends change. All things considered, we should show our love to our friends, because *A friend loves at all times…* (Proverbs 17:17). We should spend time with them, talk to them, take an interest in their lives, and in the reverse, they should do the same for us. In our church settings, we should make sure that we emphasize principles of friendship, teaching people how to be good friends and how to interact with one another in brotherly love.

Love in church

The church should be an agency of God's love to the world. Too often, as we have already discussed, it often doesn't reflect that. We have entire generations of people who have been badly and unspeakably hurt by people who were supposed to be agents of God's love. There are all sorts of reasons why this is, but none of them matter at the moment. We can understand the "why" something is done, but in the end, when it comes to love, the excuses are not viable. John 15:9-17 says:

"As the Father has loved Me, so have I loved you. Now remain in My love. If you keep My commands, you will remain in My love, just as I have kept My Father's commands and remain in His love. I have told you this so that My joy may be in you and that your joy may be complete. My command is this: Love each other as I have loved you. Greater love has no one than this: to lay down one's life for one's friends. You are My friends if you do what I command. I no longer call you servants, because a servant does not know his master's business. Instead, I have called you friends, for everything that I learned from My Father I have made known to you. You did not choose Me, but I chose you and appointed you so that you might go and bear fruit – fruit that will last – and so that whatever you ask in My Name the Father will give you. This is My command: Love each other."

If we are in church, we should be living the precepts of love we have discussed in this chapter, right unto the end that Jesus commanded us in John 15.

Leaders in the church have a unique way express love, and that is through the role of what we call "covering." Some argue that the role of covering is not Biblical, but the Bible begs to differ. Peter 4:8 tells us:

Above all, love each other deeply, because love covers over a multitude of sins.

The book of 1 Peter was written by an apostle who wrote extensively about leadership. Even though 1 Peter 4:8 is not exclusively about leaders, the remainder of the passage talks about leadership duties, especially stepping up and doing the work of the ministry (1 Peter 4:9-11). We could brush by it and think nothing of it, but I don't believe that's the intention of the passage. The passage is about love, and one of the ways that leaders love is by covering a multitude of sins, forbearing with those they cover and helping them overcome the sins that bind in their lives. It's not a leader's job to run around disgracing people but helping them to overcome and heal. It is a leader's job to love, and 1 Peter 4:8 calls out to leaders to remind them of this important fact. If leaders don't love the people they are training and raising up for the Kingdom, they won't help them to overcome the things that keep them from being all God would desire them to become.

Producing more excellent fruit

Where are you when it comes to love? Where can you do better? Here are some suggestions on ways to produce a more excellent fruit of love:

- **Study more on love, specifically *agape* love**: We've looked at love to a certain extent, but there is much, much more that can be said about love than we can present in this chapter. Do a study on love in the Bible, on the love of God, on love of neighbor, on God's love through Jesus Christ, and on the love between Christ and the Church.

- **Consider motives (and no, I don't just mean your own)**: Sometimes we work with others because we genuinely want them to like us or care about us, but we reach a point when we realize the inverse of that relationship is simply not there. Not every project, motive, church activity, conference, or work is done with love's guidance. If you have been part of something for awhile that seems good but doesn't seem to be moving anywhere, it might be time to prune back some projects or some relationships.

- **Look around with careful observations**: It is not as hard to bless other people as we might think. People tend to tell us what they like, dislike, what interests them, and what's important to them, if we will only listen. Take some initiative and do something good for someone else! Buy them a book, get them a gift card, take them out, give them a gift, help them out with some groceries, cook a meal, make them something…be creative!

- **Be part of a church fellowship that believes love is important**: Church groups might agree or disagree on politics or social issues, but the entire church should agree about love and representing God's love to the world. Even though everyone might not agree about the best way to do this, it's important to be in a church that preaches love rather than hate and avoids marginalizing certain groups or picking on certain groups from the pulpit.

- **Resist the urge to argue with others**: Whether they are non-believers or your brothers and sisters in Christ, getting into a big debate on social media is not a Christian thing to do. I know how tempting it is to start with someone who gets rude and nasty, especially if their behavior is unwarranted, but arguing with people like that doesn't change anyone's mind. If anything, it just turns everyone off…especially those who already think Christians don't know how to conduct themselves.

- **Let someone else talk for a change**: Christians like to be right and like to have the final word on everything under the sun. In this, they aren't unique from the non-believer. Everyone wants to be heard, valued, and considered for what they have to say. That being said, let someone else have the last word for a change. Take a deep breath and stop talking so much. Let others have their right to their opinions, their right to disagree, and still show them love and respect as human beings, even though their thoughts differ from yours.

- **Pray for people:** I know that sometimes we use prayer as an excuse not to really do something for others, but I'm not talking about praying in place of doing what you can. Remember, we already discussed observing needs and wants and doing something from that motivating place. I'm talking praying for others in their need because it comforts, soothes, and it gives a great way to show others the love of God without lecture or pretention. Prayer helps bridge the gap between individuals and God. It also helps us, as people, to feel connected.

Chapter Three

Joy

When the Lord restored the fortunes of Zion,
we were like those who dreamed.
Our mouths were filled with laughter,
our tongues with songs of joy.
Then it was said among the nations,
"The Lord has done great things for them."
The Lord has done great things for us,
and we are filled with joy.
— Psalm 126:1-3

Assignments:
- Read Luke 1:39-56.
- Begin the process to heal from memories that are holding you captive and stealing your joy.
- Do an activity you used to enjoy at an earlier point in your life, but you stopped doing because of "time."

When I was a kid, "joy" was a name. It was the name of a girl who attended the same city "summer rec" program as I did, every year. She was grouchy all the time because we used to call her "Joyce" by accident. I wouldn't call her my "friend," because I just didn't like her that much (nor did I know her very well). She was friends with another girl I knew (the daughter of one of my mother's friends), who was also kind of weird and sullen much of the time. Because she was friends with this other girl, we would "hang out" during Rec some of the time. It was summer, we were kids, we were not in school, we got to play in the morning and go to the pool in the afternoon, and she was still mad and out of sorts. "Joy" just didn't seem to fit her, because she never seemed…well…joyful. I can still hear her squabbling about this or that, mad about this thing or that thing, because there was always something wrong with everything. It was either not pretty enough or not sophisticated enough or not enough to her liking…I am sure you get the picture. Joy was anything but…full of joy.

I didn't know joy was a state of being because I never thought of it that way. I figured joy was being really, really happy. I didn't grow up in a church that was very joyful…or happy, at that. Much like the girl from summer rec, it felt like we found reasons not to be joyful. We were solemn, somber, and serious, even as children. Church was a time to be quiet, not to be loud or exuberant. (It's probably not a wonder that I am on the serious side in my personality.) We didn't talk about joy. We weren't encouraged to pursue joy or act joyful. Even holidays like Christmas and Easter were very somber, serious occasions when we were at church. We might have heard about it in a song or claimed someone was "full of joy," but that was the end of it.

However, among my various memories, there is one thing that stood out that relates to joy: what we used to call the *Magnificat*, better known as "Mary's Song." In what I now know to be a passage of Scripture (which we shall discuss later), Mary speaks an unending prose of gratitude and joy to God for the opportunity to be the mother of Jesus Christ, chosen for this task. I remember studying it in seventh grade religion class. We had to write it out on paper, memorize it, and decorate the page as part of a classroom project. Even though we didn't talk about it, I remember thinking how incredibly blessed Mary was at that moment, to make such a profound statement. What a moment that must have been in history! Her proclamation was great, loud, and life-changing! Surely being the mother of the Savior must have been an endless parade of happiness (there's that word again), and she must have known her life was going to forever echo the happiness of that moment.

When I got older and studied Mary's life a little more thoroughly, my perception of joy as her endless state of happiness changed dramatically. In some ways, Mary was no different than you or me, and her walk of joy wasn't that different, either. Even though she had a specific and unique call to her life, the things that defined her joy can be ours, as well…. if we let them!

What is joy?

Joy is, unfortunately, not something we talk about often. The major world's focus on happiness, which is different from joy (and I will explain the difference between the two momentarily). It is a difference that matters. If we focus on happiness instead of joy, we will never learn how to have joy, and how joy can change your life.

In trying to define joy, I wound up in the book of Ecclesiastes. Let me say, I am a huge fan of the book of Ecclesiastes. As a former philosophy major, the fact that the writer of Ecclesiastes is called "the philosopher" thrills me. In all seriousness, Ecclesiastes is a book about life written from a strictly philosophical viewpoint. It's written from the perspective of someone who has had many life experiences and wants to make sense and meaning of them all. Even though the tone of Ecclesiastes is not particularly brimming with joy or fun, there are a few important verses that give us great insight into what joy is, found in Ecclesiastes 8:14-17:

There is something else meaningless that occurs on earth: righteous who get what the wicked deserve, and wicked who get what the righteous deserve. This too, I say, is meaningless. So I commend the enjoyment of life, because there is nothing better for a person under the sun than to eat and drink and be glad. Then joy will accompany them in their toil all the days of the life God has given them under the sun.

When I applied my mind to know wisdom and to observe the labor that is done on earth – people getting no sleep day or night – then I saw all that God has done. No one can comprehend what goes on under the sun. Despite all their efforts to search it out, no one can discover its meaning. Even if the wise claim they know, they cannot really comprehend it.

> **BUD BREAKS: Joy**
> #5479 *chara*
> [khar-ah']: joy, gladness.

Through what some perceive to be complicated text, the philosopher is telling that life is meant to be lived. If we sit around and ponder on everything in the world that is wicked, wrong, evil, or seemingly unfair, we won't walk away with the answers. Instead, we will be left with a sense of emptiness. Pondering on such things incessantly, therefore, is meaningless. If we really want to find the meaning of life, we need to live life: find things we enjoy, take pleasure in simple things, and see that joy accompanies us throughout our lives. Based on this passage, we can see:

- **Joy is life lived**: Living life well isn't about having a lot of money. There are lots of people who have lots and lots of money, but they aren't joyful. Living life well is about living life in a place of contentment and satisfaction as one walks in God's will for their lives.

- **Joy is taking satisfaction in one's work**: The disgruntled worker is a staple of the modern workplace. It's common to complain about dissatisfaction on the job. There's nothing wrong with voicing a complaint about a bad day, but some do it to the point where it affects their attitude about work. Like a job or not, we should still seek to do a good job. If you want to find joy, a constantly negative attitude is a problem. It's important to like what we do, if at all possible, but whether or not we really like our job, we can do our job well to present quality work for each task. This brings a sense of purpose and satisfaction to a job well done.

> **PRUNING POINTS**: What are some things that make you happy? How do you respond when these things are not available to you? List some ways that you can start to find joy, even when the things that make you happy are not available.

- **Joy is about living in the moment and being blessed by what exists now**: It's easy to be consumed by past haunts, the things that others seem to get that you don't, to feel slighted, or to feel like you are missing something in your life. Sitting around and dwelling on such things for too long causes one to feel down and miss the great things God is doing right now. If you allow yourself to see the many blessings that are all around you, enjoying your life will be much more plausible as you live in the "right now" rather than the "might be" or "is not possible."

- **Joy is found in savoring the "little things"**: Ecclesiastes mentions taking joy in "eating and drinking." This points our attention to savoring the little things in our lives that we encounter so frequently, we don't think about them enough. We are encouraged to savor each little thing in our lives: a good meal, a favorite drink, a restful Saturday afternoon, time with good friends, a beautiful flower, a sunny day, a good book…and whatever else may inspire you, that you are able to savor, one moment at a time.

It's clear that joy is a way we approach and live our lives: with a sense of gladness and purpose, and full confidence in contentment. We must approach life itself thoughtfully and with purpose. Joy is an awareness that God is our Creator, He knows far more than we do, and ascribing to be all-knowing and all-understanding is not going to bring us to a place of contentment. This doesn't mean that we stop learning or gaining wisdom in our lives, but it does mean that we need to keep a balance on things and balance our lives with simple, little things as much as big, major contemplations to issues no human being will ever figure out in totality.

Happiness vs. joy

Unlike the word "love" which means many things in the Bible, "joy" is typically translated as "joy" or "gladness." Both indicate the same thing: a state of joyfulness or of being glad. When someone has joy, they are not relying on outside things to make them that way; it is a way they are because they see what God has done and is doing for them. The term "happy," only found a few times in the Bible, is always used to indicate a circumstance or an outside situation that brings a certain state of delight along with it. This means that to be happy, or to achieve a longer-lasting state of happy (known as happiness), one must have an outside circumstance, force, or thing to keep them in that state.

The difference between the two is, therefore, quite clear: joy doesn't rely on outside circumstances to bring about its results, while happiness does. With the modern emphasis on being happy, more and more people are constantly looking in various places to find their constant source of happiness…and many keep coming up dry. The endless cycle of finding something else to make happy, or to bring happiness, or to seek out something else new becomes long and drawn out, with people growing more and more unhappy as they try to seek things out.

God never promised we would be happy every minute of our lives. He does indicate things in this life will make us happy (Job

5:17, Proverbs 3:13-18, Esther 8:16), but He never promises that we will have a never-ending string of them to lead us to happiness. What God does promise us is that we can find joy, and that the joy of the Lord can be our never-ending source of strength and blessing in our lives.

Different ways "joy" is expressed in the Bible

There are a few different forms of the word "joy" in the Bible. These include:

- **Gladness**: The state of having joy, of being glad and content.

- **Joyful**: To be completely full of joy, so no trace of sorrow can remain therein.

- **Enjoy**: To have or be in a state of joy.

- **Rejoice**: To find joy in something all over again. For example, someone might rejoice in God because He did something amazing in their life before, and now He is doing it again. This would be a situation where joy is renewed and refreshed, both at once.

The foundational plumbing to our spiritual house

When someone builds a house, the second step of building is to install the basics of the plumbing system, right after the foundation is complete. In our fruit of the Spirit "house," joy would be the installation of the plumbing system. If we are walking in love, we will find a new joy that comes from God's eternal springs welling up inside of us (Isaiah 12:3). Joy can be turned on or shut off, and if we have sprung a leak or joy is not channeling properly in our lives, it comes at a cost.

Living in joy is a choice we make. It doesn't just happen because we hope something falls out of the sky to make our lives perfect or right. Just like when we decide to take a shower and we turn on the faucet connected to the shower head in the bathroom, we must turn on to joy in our lives. In many instances, it requires us to completely rethink the things in our lives that are the most ordinary or "boring" to us and examine our attitudes about performing everyday tasks. It also requires healing, so we can come to a place of freedom from things that hinder us from walking in joy.

Joy and healing

Every person on this planet has things in their lives that require healing. Most of us have a few things that would be considered "major" areas for healing, and then we have some issues that would be considered more "minor" by nature. The difference between a major thing for healing and a minor one is the level of hold the issue has over our lives. A major issue might seriously impact our ability to live normally: hold down a job, have friends or intimate relationships with others, meet with familial responsibilities, pay bills, or interact with others in society. Minor issues don't hamper the major day-to-day living of an individual, but may hamper personal advancement, growth, or other interactions with others. Different issues affect different people in different ways. Someone who might have been seriously abused as a child or in an intimate relationship as an adult might have serious issues with personal relationships but might be great at their job. Someone who is a wild tale-telling gossip might have trouble keeping a job because they get fired all the time. It's not so much what the issue is that the person needs to heal from as the way it affects their life, and the way it affects their interactions with others.

> **HAPPY HARVEST:** What are you going through right now that could use a jolt of joy? Keep joy as a focal point as you work toward healing in your life!

Being bound by an issue is never a fun experience. People who have been in prison for extended periods of time talk about how isolating, lonely, and uncomfortable the experience is. It is one that the incarcerated never fully adjust to, no matter how many years they might be in prison. The same is true for people who are bound by their hurts, haunts, pasts, and experiences. There are millions of people walking this earth who might very well have enough of Jesus in their lives to go to heaven when they die, but not have allowed Him to move in their lives enough to experience a joy-filled life. It's impossible to walk in joy and walk in the confines of bondages that limit our ability to experience contentment and appreciate the things we have in this life that we can be grateful for.

Thus, healing is needed to walk in joy. We need to accept the love of God to transform the deep hurts and offenses we have experienced and move forward in our lives. We need to let God do what He wants to do within us, changing our ways and patterns of thinking, our attitudes about ourselves and our lives, and our attitudes about other people.

We talk often about the spiritual gift of healing and what a great thing it is to have. People seek to have this gift, even to the point of lying about having it. What we don't talk about is that receiving healing in one's life is also a gift, and a profound spiritual one, at that. Healing, as a process, begins when we have that moment when we decide to let God have His chance to make things right for us. They won't ever be the way they used to be, but they will be something else, something more meaningful, something beyond what we can imagine for ourselves.

If you need healing, there are many ways to accomplish it. Prayer, services specifically for healing, counseling or therapy, talking to trusted friends, support groups, and daily spiritual disciplines can help to bring about the work of healing in your life. If you truly want to find joy, finding healing is the first step to bringing that about. Each step you take to get free is one more step you will have in finding joy.

In Psalm 16:5-11, David recounts the following words that related powerfully to a healing process he himself experienced, finding joy on the other side:

LORD, *You alone are my portion and my cup;*
  You make my lot secure.
The boundary lines have fallen for me in pleasant places;
  surely I have a delightful inheritance.

I will praise the LORD, Who counsels me;
  even at night my heart instructs me.
I keep my eyes always on the LORD.
  With Him at my right hand, I will not be shaken.

Therefore my heart is glad and my tongue rejoices;
  my body also will rest secure,
because You will not abandon me to the realm of the dead,
  nor will You let Your faithful One see decay.
You have made known to me the path of life;
  You will fill me with joy in Your presence,
  with eternal pleasures at Your right hand.

We know from Scripture that David experienced repentance and healing many times in his life. He did not do everything right, he suffered from familial rejections and experienced deaths in his family, and he needed the Lord's restoration to be whole and healed so he could rightly lead the nation of Israel. David's work as a leader was so profound because He constantly allowed God to work in him unto the end of healing and, ultimately, joy. Part of David's success was knowing God was the source of his joy, and he could overcome his circumstances to find joy in everything he did.

Attributes of joy

In the first part of this chapter, I spoke on Mary's Song, known in high church circles as the *Magnificat*. This important passage of Scripture is seldom studied but is an excellent example of joy and the expression of joy in one's life, especially when we consider what Mary went through in her life as the mother of Jesus.

Luke 1:39-45:

At that time Mary got ready and hurried to a town in the hill country of Judea, where she entered Zechariah's home and greeted Elizabeth. When Elizabeth heard Mary's greeting, the baby leaped in her womb, and Elizabeth was filled with the Holy Spirit. In a loud voice she exclaimed: "Blessed are you among women, and blessed is the child you will bear! But why am I so favored, that the mother of my Lord should come to me? As soon as the sound of your greeting reached my ears, the baby in my womb leaped for joy. Blessed is she who has believed that what the Lord would fulfill His promises to her!"

Right before this passage we read about Mary's encounter with the angel Gabriel. He came with the message that her life was about to change forever: she was chosen to become the mother of the Savior of the world, Jesus Christ. I would say that after that news, you would want some time to contemplate how life was going to change. Mary's trip to visit Elizabeth wasn't just to meditate on the wonders that were to come, but to protect her from an invading world that wasn't so embracing, nor celebratory, about her news. Regardless of the outside world – which would be dealt with at a later time – we see two women who are full of joy because of what God has done for and through them.

In this joy-filled moment, we see the supernatural at work. Mary and Elizabeth shared their joy, and even John the Baptist who was not yet born leaped for joy! Elizabeth (a woman) was the first person in the Scriptures who was filled with the Holy Spirit. When she was filled with the Holy Spirit, she spoke loudly, proclaiming the greatness of God and celebrating the blessing in Mary that she was to be the mother of the Savior. Joy came forth because both Mary and Elizabeth believed in God for their completely impossible situations. Mary was a virgin and was not in position to have a baby, and Elizabeth was past child-bearing years and previously unable to conceive. From one barren womb and one unfruitful womb came a prophet and our Emmanuel!

Luke 1:46-56:

And Mary said:
   My soul glorifies the Lord
     and my spirit rejoices in God my Savior,
for He has been mindful
   of the humble state of His servant.
From now on all generations will call me blessed,
for the Mighty One has done great things for me –
   holy is His Name.
His mercy extends to those who fear Him,

from generation to generation.
He has performed mighty deeds with His arm;
  He has scattered those who are proud in their inmost thoughts.
He has brought down rulers from their thrones
  but has lifted up the humble.
He has filled the hungry with good things
  but has sent the rich away empty.
He has helped His servant Israel,
  remembering to be merciful
to Abraham and his descendants forever,
  just as He promised our ancestors."

Mary stayed with Elizabeth for about three months and then returned home.

Mary's expression of joy was certainly not an expression of happiness. Most don't consider that Mary was nothing more than a young pubescent girl when the angel Gabriel came and gave her this incredible news. She's going to be the mother of the Savior of the world! Her fiancé, Joseph, is ready to divorce her because he automatically assumes the worst of her. I'm sure people around town were not readily accepting of her version of the events that had transpired. There would forever be rumors and speculation surrounding her morals and character. Mary lived with the reality that she would forever have a son that would never be hers beyond her biology, because His call would forever be greater than that of this world. She would never watch Him get married or have grandchildren from her first-born. Joseph would forever live with a child that was not his biological child, and I believe that was never a thought that escaped his mind. Her life was never going to take the ordinary course that she expected it would. Now, too, Mary was always going to be different. Mary had many tasks, challenges, and

> **POLLINATION POINTS:** Mary and Elizabeth brought each other a sense of encouragement that led to an overwhelming experience of joy. Get together with some trusted prayer partners, especially ones you haven't talked to in awhile...and watch God's joy explode on the scene!

issues ahead of her that would not always leave her happy. She would have times, like any mother, where she was tired of doing the same thing repeatedly. She would find the days when her Son was taken from her and killed to be unbearable. She would, once again, rejoice when He came back to life, but in the meantime…Mary's life was still, no longer, her own.

Mary didn't just rejoice (find joy all over again) in God because of what He had done for her, but because of what He did, faithful to His Word, for generations. Mary recognized God is the source of all joy, not just her own. His mindfulness, mercy, mighty deeds, humbling of the proud, changing paradigms, filling the hungry, and helping His servants throughout history were all things we can celebrate, because we are all a part of them. If you are a part of God's Kingdom, you are a part of a long lineage, you, too, are a part of this joy!

Joy's major attributes are thankfulness, gratitude, glory and honor. Mary knew all glory went to God, and she would glorify Him in her joy. She was thankful, grateful, honoring, humble, and proud to serve her God, Who she knew would always come through for her and carry her through when necessary. If we want to be joyful, we must trust God.

EnJOY life

One of the things we should see in Mary's song is the way in which she celebrated God in many ordinary ways. She rejoiced in God in her everyday life and the way she saw and knew Him to be faithful. She didn't just celebrate God because He sent her a new car or because He overthrew the Roman government. Mary knew that, as hard as life was at times, it was worth enjoying. She had the option to rush through her life, try to get her engagement moving and save her reputation, or to try and get Jesus to grow up faster than He was going to grow up, or spend her entire life trying to arrange her life in addition to God's arrangements, but Mary didn't do that. Instead, she enjoyed each moment as best as she could, cherishing things in her heart (Luke 2:19).

Thus, the inevitable question for you: do you know how to enjoy life?

There's an anonymous poem I heard some years back that I feel summarizes the way too many people approach life today:

First, I was dying to finish high school and start college.
And then I was dying to finish college and start working.
And then I was dying to marry and have children.
And then I was dying for my children to grow old enough for school so I could return to work.
And then I was dying to retire.
And now I am dying...
And suddenly I realize I forgot to live.[1]

It seems like our world is always in a "rush" to get to the next phase of life. I meet many people who are in a constant hurry to get to whatever's next for them. They don't like waiting and they don't like slowing things down and waiting to see where they go. People rush through different stages of life, people push and force things to happen out of season and before their time, and they are always on the fast-track, looking for that new job, relationship, phase of the relationship, days off, weekend time, next conference, next promotion, new baby, kids out of the house...I am sure you get the picture. The excessive states of discontent and dissatisfaction permeates through people's lives as they look for the next thing or the new thing to make them happy.

> **FOUNDATIONAL FERTILIZER:** I was once intensely pursued by a man who barely knew me but wanted to talk marriage after we had talked on the phone one time and exchanged a few emails. His insistence that he wanted to rush – rush here, rush there, move things along – had to do with his own past experiences in relationships, causing him to want to skip over essential things like discussion and getting to know one another. This ensured we would never be more involved, because he didn't give me the opportunity to get to know him as a person and decide if he was right for me. In what ways are you trying to "rush" around your life? How can you slow down a bit to enjoy life more?

I think the first thing we need to think about in this instance is…slowing down! This fast-track thinking is not helping anyone to enjoy anything! We rush through meals, classes, services, relationships, jobs, and moments, only to have life completely pass us by. It is not God's will that we, as human beings, move so fast. Just as Mary recognized the great things and the little things God had done and was doing, we need to stop only looking to "help God out" with big things. Rushing through life isn't going to make God move any faster on our behalf, it is just going to make sure that we miss out on all the little things He has given to us to make life enjoyable.

There are so many who rushed through steps and stages of life and now wish they had some of them back. Many married people miss the earlier phases of courtship, where the relationship was more about fun and enjoyment and less about working on a relationship all the time. So many people wish they had enjoyed their single years more, or their years as a young couple with no children. Older people wish they had enjoyed their children more when they were young. Preachers with larger congregations miss their smaller, more intimate audiences. People with complex lives miss their simpler days. Whatever it is, so much rushing creates lack of contentment and dissatisfaction with life.

Even in the state of a malcontent, the Lord reaches out to us and reminds us in Isaiah 49:13:

Shout for joy, you heavens;
  rejoice, you earth;
  burst into song, you mountains!
For the LORD comforts His people
  and will have compassion on His afflicted ones.

Joy is the ultimate confidence that God's 'got us,' as we would say. If we would only take time to see Him move in our lives, we would find the contentment we seek.

The fullness of joy

In John 16:19-24, Jesus tells us:

Jesus saw that they wanted to ask Him about this, so He said to them, "Are you asking one another what I meant when I said, 'In a little while you will see Me no more, and then after a little while you will see Me'? Very truly I tell you, you will weep and mourn while the world rejoices. You will grieve, but your grief will turn to joy. A woman giving birth to a child has pain because her time has come; but when her baby is born she forgets the anguish because of her joy that a child is born into the world. So with you: Now is your time of grief, but I will see you again and you will rejoice, and no one will take away your joy. In that day you will no longer ask Me anything. Very truly I tell you, My Father will give you whatever you ask in My Name. Until now you have not asked for anything in My Name. Ask and you will receive, and your joy will be complete."

> **FOUNDATIONAL FERTILIZER:** When I was first in ministry, I was always in a big hurry. I hated that my ministry always seemed stagnant and unable to go beyond a certain level with whatever I was doing. I hated the disciplines I went through, often daily: Highlighting and underlining every passage in the Bible in a color-coded system the Lord gave to me, praying, talking to people online, preparing messages, and starting church. Now that I am many more years into this than I was then, with many more responsibilities, I realize what a gift I had all those years ago, while I was developing a deeper walk with the Lord that I would need to do what I do today. What do you despise right now that is essential and foundational to the things God wants to do in your life?

Being a person that leads a joy-filled life means finding that purpose in Jesus Christ. If we find our purpose in Him, we aren't as apt to rush through everything we encounter.

Through healing, slowing down, and enjoying everything life has to offer a little more, the fullness of joy that Jesus promised us is ours for the taking. We have the authority to pray in His Name and seek God for a cessation of internal strife and a better direction for a life full of joy. Praise His Name and seek His face, for He will guide you. Honor and put God first in all things, and He will bring you to a place where joy will never lack, no matter how hard of a time you might experience.

Producing more excellent fruit

Where are you when it comes to joy? Where can you do better? Here are some suggestions on ways to produce a more excellent fruit of joy:

- **Study more about the history of psalmistry and songwriting throughout the ages**: Singing to God as we offer God the fruit of our lips through musical praise is a long historical tradition. It is fascinating and inspiring, both at the same time. There is so much we can say about the concept of being able to express our joy for the Lord in music, and the different circumstances that brought about the songs of joy throughout the ages. Learn more about the principle of rejoicing, review the Psalms, and sing along with your own magnificent song that echoes down through the ages. Check out some older songs as well as newer ones and hear the joy of the Lord strengthen believers from the past to the present through your own worship.

- **Remember the little things that used to bring you joy**: Too often we abandon things that used to bring us joy because we don't feel we have time for them anymore. If you don't have time for things that inspire joy, you are too busy! Think of some of the things you used to enjoy and make the effort to do some of them again. If you can't do them every day, do them from time to time, to inspire wonder and awe back into your life.

- **Spend some time outside**: I'm sure from earlier chapters you'll be shocked to learn I am not personally an outdoorsy girl. I don't like the great outdoors as a rule. I told my husband outright I refuse to do things like go camping. But I can't deny that getting outside for a walk, going to the beach for an afternoon, or standing outside under a night sky sometimes fills me with a sense of awe and wonder about what God is doing in both my life, and the lives of many others I know. Since God is our Creator, beholding His creation connects us to Him and fills us with a sense of joy and excitement, because creation is an incredible thing.

- **Do something creative**: Echoing the point I just made about creation, God has endowed us with the ability to be creative, as well. Even though we run amuck with science to the exclusion of the arts in schools, the creative arts help to connect us to God in an active prophetic manner. Participating in creation is to participate in prophecy, as the natural world is an example of the amazing things God did by His Word alone. The things we do by creativity create a motor memory within us, associating what we do with the way we feel when we are doing it. Whether painting, drawing, dance, music, song, poetry, writing, building items, or another creative art, creativity helps connect us all to the Creator and gives us a sense of joy as pertains to creating new things.

- **Laugh more**: At some point in history, church people got the message that laughing is bad and looking like you just sucked on a lime is good. Being uptight, stoic, unhappy, and somber all the time is not the way God intends us to be! Relax some! It's all right to find things funny, to have a good sense of humor, even to enjoy some comedic things from time to time. Laughing helps us have a better sense of joy about things, especially in difficult situations.

- **Do something just for fun**: It's perfectly all right to have fun and be a Christian. While we might not find some forms of entertainment to be appropriate for us anymore, there is nothing wrong with enjoying yourself as you have a good time.

- **Spend time with others**: In my ministry, it's difficult for all the churches and ministries I cover to get together in one sitting. This means the time we spend together is all the more important. Don't isolate yourself or become an island away from everyone else. These new movements that discourage people from going to church and from spending time with other believers are bad, not to mention unscriptural. Spend time with others to build up your own faith and, yes, increase your own joy.

References
[1] http://www.boardofwisdom.com/togo/Quotes/ShowQuote/?msgid=7967#.VUgBzpMamjE. Accessed May 4, 2015.

Chapter Four

Peace

"THE LORD BLESS YOU
AND KEEP YOU;
THE LORD MAKE HIS FACE SHINE ON YOU
AND BE GRACIOUS TO YOU;
THE LORD TURN HIS FACE TOWARD YOU
AND GIVE YOU PEACE."
– NUMBERS 6:24-26

Assignments:
- Read Ephesians 2:11-22.
- Sit quietly and meditate on a Scripture passage with special meaning to you for at least ten minutes, uninterrupted, with no distractions.
- Finish a project you've been putting off for a long time.

In the 1980s, people were afraid nuclear war would break out and obliterate the entire human race. Songs about peace and prayers encouraging peace were common. School children wrote letters to their government officials, urging for peace and a cessation of war. There was outrage among the citizens of several nations who could not believe their leaders would be willing to disrupt world peace and a sense of good will among the nations in the name of causing such trouble. Nuclear weapons became the ultimate threat and concern as humanity felt it was the ultimate way we would destroy humanity.

If the last several thousand years of human history are any clue, nuclear weapons will have to get in line when it comes to our ability to self-destruct. Wars, conflicts, violence, abuse, misuse, selfishness, and discord have all contributed to the lack of peace in this world. Unable to discuss and solve our conflicts with better methods, the world has long resorted to inhumanity, taking lives and abusing others, and being generally disruptive along the way. Humanity can take itself out, without any help needed from nuclear sources.

This is why peace is such a prized thing, especially when we start talking about national and international peace: it's rare. Seldom in history has the entire world ever been at total peace. With nations come threats to what we now perceive to be national security, and with those threats comes a sense of defensiveness that calls up the battle to mount and defend, even if the threat is null and void.

I think the fact that Jesus spoke so much about peace in the context of the Kingdom of God is fascinating, especially since the Bible indicates He did not walk among men in peaceful times.

Israel's Roman occupation led many of His followers to be violent revolutionaries who needed to reorient their entire way of looking at the world and looking at ways to handle issues and conflicts. Jesus advocated peace, while also teaching us about spiritual battle and that life would not always be as peaceful around us as we might hope. Despite the fact that the world might not always measure up to our hopes of peace, Jesus still told us that peace is something we can aspire to, and achieve.

What do you think of when you think of peace? Do you think of a lake, quiet and tranquil, in late summer? Do you think of the world after a cease fire is declared at the end of a war? Do you think of a monastery, bathed in complete silence as everyone works? Is it sitting down at the end of a long, hard day without any disruptions and a cold drink in your hand? Peace is much, much more than any of these things. In fact, it is, once again, a part of the fruit of the Spirit that the believer must grow in so we are better able to withstand the things we will encounter in this life.

> **BUD BREAKS: Peace**
> #1515 *eirene* [i-ray'-nay]: 1) a state of national tranquility 2) peace between individuals, i.e. harmony, concord 3) security, safety, prosperity, felicity, (because peace and harmony make and keep things safe and prosperous) 4) of the Messiah's peace 5) of Christianity, the tranquil state of a soul assured of its salvation through Christ, and so fearing nothing from God and content with its earthly lot, of whatsoever sort that is 6) the blessed state of devout and upright men after death.

What is peace?

It's hard to define peace without defining what it is not. Peace is the opposite of conflict and discord. It's a place of tranquility, harmony, safety, security, and the open door to all the things that come when things are in a situation that lacks strife and conflict.

The Greek and Hebrew terms for "peace" differ slightly. In the Greek, the term for "peace" reflects the absence of conflict. The Hebrew word for peace, often transliterated as *shalom*, first defines it as completeness and soundness. This tells us that peace begins within, with completeness and soundness of body, mind, soul, and spirit. Understanding this makes it easier to see peace as a plausible entity, even if the world is disrupted.

1 Peter 3:8-17 tells us a lot about peace.

Finally, all of you, be like-minded, be sympathetic, love one another, be compassionate and humble. Do not repay evil with evil or insult with insult. On the contrary, repay evil with blessing, because to this you were called so that you may inherit a blessing. For,

> *"Whoever would love life*
> *and see good days*
> *must keep their tongue from evil*
> *and their lips from deceitful speech.*
> *They must turn from evil and do good;*
> *they must seek peace and pursue it.*
> *For the eyes of the Lord are on the righteous*
> *and His ears are attentive to their prayer,*
> *but the face of the Lord is against those who do evil."*

Who is going to harm you if you are eager to do good? But even if you should suffer for what is right, you are blessed. "Do not fear their threats; do not be frightened." But in your hearts revere Christ as Lord. Always be prepared to give an answer to everyone who asks you to give the reason for the hope that you have. But do this with gentleness and respect, keeping a clear conscience, so that those who speak maliciously against your good behavior will be ashamed of their slander. For it is better, if it is God's will, to suffer for doing good than for doing evil.

From this, we learn the following:

- **Peace begins with our own personal reconciliations toward harmony**: Someone must be willing to make harmony in conflict-ridden situations. That means we must reflect the values that are stated above, including sympathy, brotherly love, compassion, and humility.

- **Peace stops repaying evil for evil (or "getting even" with others)**: The endless cycle of trying to rectify situations by getting back at others who have wronged us must end somewhere, with someone. If you strive for peace in your life, you will be the one who ends that cycle. Revenge sounds fun, it sounds like it will make you feel better, but it just starts an endless parade of tit for tat: where you do something and someone else does something and so on…forever and ever…sometimes into multiple generations.

- **Peace forgives**: If we stop repaying evil for evil, we forgive others, just as in Christ, God has forgiven us (Ephesians 4:32, Colossians 3:13). If you want peace, you are going to have to let some things go and let God deal with you and the people in your life who have wronged you, so you can be free.

- **Peace conducts itself uprightly**: Behaving uprightly relates to personal speech, conduct, and attitude. Our interactions with others should be handled with grace and poise, without inciting argument or improper behavior. In all things, we do unto others as we would have them do unto us (Matthew 7:12, Luke 6:31). Yes, sometimes people's behaviors need to be addressed, and sometimes they don't respond to it well, but that is not helped by unseemly aggression and nasty attitudes. In peace, we remember that we don't have to stoop to the world's level to make our point.

> **BUD BREAKS: Peace**
> #7965 *shalowm* /shaw-lome'] or *shalom* [shaw-lome']: completeness, soundness, welfare, peace.

- **Peace is, in and of itself, a blessing**: Peace is very sought out in today's world. People will spend thousands of dollars to jet off to Tibet, contort their bodies trying to do yoga, meditate on all sorts of non-Christian deities, and do many other things to try and de-clutter their mental space and soothe emotional wounds. The Scriptures don't indicate we have to do so many far-reaching things to find peace. They do promise that once we've found our peace in Christ (John 16:33, Philippians 4:7), we have found something powerful that the world cannot take away.

- **Peace must be sought and pursued**: We don't discover peace because it falls on our heads. It doesn't just randomly walk up to us one day. We find peace when we turn away from evil and seek to do good. We must seek out peace and make the effort to turn from sinful ways, avoid doing things that are reactive, and deliberately apply God's principles to each situation. Rather than chase after our own way, we need to chase the peaceful solution to situations.

- **Peace and fear do not mix**: As people, we are wired to respond in fear. We see every negative remark, aggressive behavior, and unkind action as personal attacks toward us. In our minds, we perceive such to be threats to our lives in some fashion. If we want to be peaceful people, we must put down our fearfully aggressive tendencies and pick up spiritual responses (Matthew 5:38-40). Rather than viewing everyone as an enemy, we must see things through peaceful eyes and look upon others with compassion and love (Matthew 9:36-38, Luke 10:30-35, Colossians 3:12, 1 Peter 3:8).

- **Peace acknowledges Christ as Lord** – Christ is the center of our lives, hope, and work. In the face of opposition, violent protests, and angry leaders, He remained peaceful and confident, knowing His Father was with Him. If we want to know peace, we must know the Prince of Peace, Jesus Christ.

- **Peace is prepared**: We grow flustered when we don't have an answer, especially if it's to an important question. It is easy to grow frantic, angry, and conflicted when we don't know what to say. As much as is possible, we should realize that learning and knowledge help us be prepared with answers when questions arise. Additionally, the Spirit of God can intervene for us in the gap when we are unsure of something in the natural realm.

- **Peace is respectful**: There is no reason to be rude or virulent with speech or conduct. As Christians, we are called to be people who respect life. We do this, not because people are always lovable, but because God's image is found within others (Genesis 1:1). Even if we don't particularly hold a lot of respect for an individual, we still can maintain respect for God, because that is a person He has created (Genesis 1:27).

- **Peace keeps a clear conscience**: Evildoers will never find the peace they might appear to have (Psalm 37:1). While someone who is deliberately doing wrong might seem to be doing all right in their lives, they can never know true peace. If we want to be peaceful, we need to seek to do good, rather than evil, in our lives. Our conscience must remain clear as we pursue the things important to us in this life.

- **Peace suffers with a good attitude**: This is probably the part of peace most difficult to understand. You can be the best person in the world, and you will still have to go through some things in this life that will equate to personal "suffering." It may not be as intense or difficult as others in the world, but it will still be hard for you to endure. If we are people of peace, we can go through these difficult periods in our lives with a good attitude, trusting in God to transform our situations as we grow and go through things we would rather not.

Different ways the word peace is used in the Bible

Peace is used to indicate different things in the Bible, both within us and outside of us.

- **National peace**: Indicates a nation (usually ancient Israel) was at peace, without disruption, internal fighting, or international war. Times of peace were often periods of prosperity, because the nation was able to focus on things other than defense.

- **Political peace**: Indicates that fighting has ceased between nations. More than just honoring a ceasefire, the nations are able to keep economic ties to one another and also able to respect laws and borders without hostility, overthrow, or attack.

- **To make peace (as in being a peacemaker)**: We will talk more about peacemakers later in this chapter, but people who are able to make peace bring a sense of tranquility with them as well as a sense of wholeness and completeness to any situation.

> **FOUNDATIONAL FERTILIZER:** I once had an assistant that I literally took off the street so he would not be homeless. For almost a year, I extended myself in help and assistance to him, even though helping him caused disruption in my life and ministry. In the weeks leading up to his departure from our ministry, I knew, by many signs, such was approaching. I told God the way things were going, I couldn't keep working with him. When he finally decided to move on without our assistance, I had complete peace about his decision. While I did not care for the way he departed (as he did so in a disordered fashion), I was perfectly fine with the fact that he was gone. I know I had peace, because working with him for such a long time had been so absent of peace. What circumstances have you been in that lacked peace?

- **Prosperity**: If people are lacking in some way, it is hard to maintain peace. Prosperity here does not relate to money as much as it does to quality of life and the way that one's life is lived. It is the pursue and achievement of a whole and balanced life where one can fully provide for one's needs.

- **Restoration**: Restoration relates to healing, wholeness, wellness, and well-being. It also relates to our relationship with God in a big way. Sin destroyed our relationship with God; Jesus restored our relationship with Him. In restoration, we find completion.

- **Health**: We all know the Bible tells us we should prosper as our souls prosper. This relates to our physical health. It is God's will for His people to be healthy and to have bodies restored as much as possible this side of heaven, recovering from any ailments and walking in true victory physically as well as spiritually.

- **Rest/tranquility**: Peace relates to a well-rested state as well as tranquil, or settled, states of being.

- **Making amends**: The one most difficult for most of us, peace also relates to making amends. No matter how much we might want to try and attain peace all on our own, peace intimately relates to our interactions with others. If we are to be peaceful people, we need to know when to walk forward and when it is time to admit we were wrong and try to make amends.

The framing for our spiritual house

If love is the foundation and joy is the plumbing system, then peace is the frame of our fruit of the Spirit house. Peace is a powerful choice as framing because the frame of a house keeps the walls and floors in place. If we don't have the right frame, we can't have the right walls and the right fixtures to keep out wrong things and keep in right things. Peace is our frame, because it does just that: it protects against the storms of the world and it keeps the serenity of God in, right where it needs to be in a centering place within people's lives. It keeps us standing strong, complete, and our lives whole.

Blessed are the peacemakers...

We live in a world driven by competition and aggression. The basic message we receive throughout life is that success equates to outdoing everyone else. We are encouraged to strive for more, obtain more, have more things than other people, and have the most power. This competitive edge has caused us to lack peace. We think everyone is our enemy and out to get us, and we need to get them before they get us.

As much as we might want peace, it's an opposing view to everything we've learned throughout life. Even though the word "peace" is thrown around here and there in casual conversation (and is heard during wartime or times of international conflict) it is not found in many places or among many people. Peace, however, is something that is needed within as much as without. It also seems like very few people know and understand how to make peace a priority and take that initial first step to bring peace to a situation.

Then one day, we read Scripture (or hear a sermon) and note Jesus talks to us about being peacemakers in Matthew 5:9:

Blessed are the peacemakers,
 for they will be called sons of God.

How can we be peacemakers if we don't understand the concept of peace in general?

When I think of "peacemakers," I think of people who were involved in the cessation of war, such as Dag Hammarskjöld or Clara Barton. It's hard to think of us, in our everyday lives, as peacemakers. Where do we begin?

Let's start by saying that peacemaking is different from peace keeping. Some associate the idea of making peace with passivity:

not ever causing controversy, not making any waves, and making sure other people are always happy with us. This might sound ideal, but what this situation creates is idolatry. The more you try to please everyone else, the less you will find yourself able to hear from God, thus ending the idea of peace in your life.

At the same time, peace does not need to have your way all the time, either. If I was to describe it in this setting, it's the absence of a need to hold control over everything, all the time. Our sense of fear drives us to control, but peacemakers know when to let go for the sake of moving forward. In so doing, peacemakers are led by God in situations as how to best handle things when matters arise. A peacemaker puts God first; a peacekeeper puts people first.

The world needs peacemakers. A peacemaker, following God's will, sees the end of peace in each and every situation. Peace begins with us and with our attempt to stand as agents of the healing we have received from God rather than trying to outdo or offend other people at each and every turn.

Jesus doesn't just call us to be peacemakers; He declares peacemakers to be "blessed." They are blessed because they have embraced the blessing that peace is to them. They recognize God, even when His presence in a situation may not seem obvious. Peace is a blessing to have, and a blessing to advocate for in all things. It takes maturity to walk in peace, because it requires growth to allow God to move in one's life and through it, too. This is especially true when faced with circumstances riddled with difficulties.

> **PRUNING POINTS:** What hostilities do you still hold dear, even though Jesus has abolished them? Think of some ways you can abolish them within yourself, since Christ already abolished them on the cross.

Attributes of peace

Most of us don't think of Ephesians 2:11-22 when we think about peace. This is unfortunate, because it gives us great insight into the work of peace that Jesus desires to do within the church. The church herself is an institution created to bring reconciliation between different groups of people who were at odds before the work of Christ on the cross. Part of the church's mission is to bring peace wherever we go, inviting and maintaining peace in the global church and in each one of our individual churches, as well.

Ephesians 2:11-13:

Therefore, remember that formerly you who are Gentiles by birth and called "uncircumcised" by those who call themselves "the circumcision" (which is done in the body by human hands) – remember that at that time you were separate from Christ, excluded from citizenship in Israel and foreigners to the covenants of the promise, without hope and without God in the world. But now in Christ Jesus you who once were far away have been brought near through the blood of Christ.

At one time, every one of us was alienated from God and unable to achieve peace by our own means. We might have looked for exterior things to bring us that peace or been at enmity with other groups that had an appearance of peace (even if they, in reality, did not have it). The reason we were unable to achieve this promise is because we lived without peace – we were people without hope, and without God. The good news is that even though we were once far away, we have now been brought near, thanks to the work of Christ.

Ephesians 2:14-18:

For He Himself is our peace, Who has made the two groups one and has destroyed the barrier, the dividing wall of hostility, by setting aside in His flesh the law with its commandments and regulations. His purpose was to create in Himself one new humanity out of the two, thus making peace, and in one body to reconcile both of them to God through the cross, by which He put to death their hostility. He came and preached peace to you who were far away and peace to those who were near. For through Him we both have access to the Father by one Spirit.

Jesus Himself is our peace, because He is the perfect (Psalm 37:37) that we seek to follow unto the end of peaceful reconciliation. If we are willing to follow and embrace Christ, we can move into a place where we will find peace. Prior to the work of Christ on the cross, peace was something out of reach. The major point we need to see:

the primary attribute of peace is reconciliation, thus putting an end to hostility. What does that mean for us? It means that the overly aggressive nature that seeks to outdo others and sees every other person as a threat must be put aside. All hostile behaviors and attempts to try and outdo others or prove superior in the natural must cease.

We are surrounded by hostilities in this world. Some of the more common ones include:

- Racism and bigotry
- Sexism
- Discrimination
- Hate crimes
- Child abuse
- Domestic violence
- Assault
- Queerphobia

This passage tells us if we are truly people of peace, the nature or proclivity to do these things will also be put to death within us. We should be people who seek to do things by the spirit of God, not behaving as we might have at one point in time. Now, we seek to embrace others and reject the ways of the world that are listed above. These lead to enmity and hostility, while God's peace is contrary to and the opposite of these different matters.

Ephesians 2:19-22:

Consequently, you are no longer foreigners and strangers, but fellow citizens with God's people and also members of His household, built on the foundation of the apostles and prophets, with Christ Jesus Himself as the chief cornerstone. In Him the whole building is joined together and rises to become a holy temple in the Lord. And in Him you too are being built together to become a dwelling in which God lives by His Spirit.

Peace brings people together. It joins us, one to another, in unity with the absence of hostility. We can focus on Kingdom things and build up the work of the Spirit, one to another, as siblings in Christ. Bottom line of peace: it is the foundation to unity and solidarity in the church.

Forgiveness and peace

It's important to realize that, in studying peace, we will never reach the place of peace if we do not practice forgiveness in our lives. While a topic of controversy that is often misunderstood and improperly taught, forgiveness is essential to living a life of peace. Just as we discussed earlier, the work of Christ on the cross was one of reconciliation; it reconciled human beings back to God. It also reconciled them, one to another. The means by which this was accomplished was through forgiveness, because through Christ, we are forgiven. We can't even begin to talk about the essence of peace without talking about forgiveness, because peace is the result of forgiveness. Ephesians 1:7-10 says:

In Him we have redemption through His blood, the forgiveness of sins, in accordance with the riches of God's grace that He lavished on us. With all wisdom and understanding, He made known to us the mystery of His will according to His good pleasure, which He purposed in Christ, to be put into effect when the times reach their fulfillment – to bring unity to all things in heaven and on earth together under Christ.

> **POLLINATION POINTS:** How can you better facilitate a sense of peace and unity within your own congregation? What specific behaviors can you change that will help you be a better Christian and a better member of Christ's body?

Under that Lordship, that heavenly fulfillment, that promise of the Kingdom, we find our ultimate answer to peace. As we are forgiven, so too we must forgive, so we can rest in His peace.

Unity and peace

The church has spent years trying to stir up warm, feel-good fuzziness by throwing around talk of "unity." Sometimes the direction of the discussions are nauseating, at best, and insincere, at worst. All you have to do is say the word "unity" and people start nodding in agreement, saying what an important value it is and how sad it is that the church today does not have it.

"Sad" is the wrong word. The fact that we are using unity to try and generate attention or warm feelings is spiritually inappropriate. It shows we don't understand our role in unity. The reason we do not have unity in the church is because we are using the work of the church to further worldly hostilities and influence worldly politics rather than becoming agents of peace. If we refuse to pick up His love and put down our hostilities, we will never achieve church unity. We can't have unity without peace. No matter how many years of councils, assemblies, forums, and discussions we have, we are not going to generate peace from them. Romans 12:17-21 tells us:

Do not repay anyone evil for evil. Be careful to do what is right in the eyes of everyone. If it is possible, as far as it depends on you, live at peace with everyone. Do not take revenge, my dear friends, but leave room for God's wrath, for it is written: "It is Mine to avenge; I will repay," says the Lord. On the contrary:

> *"If your enemy is hungry, feed him;*
> *if he is thirsty, give him something to drink.*
> *In doing this, you will heap burning coals on his head."*

Do not be overcome by evil but overcome evil with good.

If the church will bring itself to follow this advice (all of which relates to peace and manifesting peace), then we will see the unity we often seek, but do not fine. We cannot use church to repay evil to other people, do wrong, or live with discord. Church is not about revenge, but about destroying that kind of enmity and keeping it from infiltrating the church. We overcome evil with good as we agree to live peaceably with others.

Peace and spiritual warfare

Modern teachings on spiritual warfare cause church members (and even fringe church attendees) to take on an almost militant characteristic in their faith. The result is a frenzied approach to matters, looking for a witch or a demon around every corner, and being suspect of other people and their motives. It's obvious that the over-emphasis on spiritual warfare is causing people to lose their perspective on life and, by extension, also lose their peace. If you are in a constant frenzy of paranoia, you can't ever experience God's peace.

Romans 8:6 tells us:

The mind governed by the flesh is death, but the mind governed by the Spirit is life and peace.

Further, Romans 15:13 says:

May the God of hope fill you with all joy and peace as you trust in Him, so that you may overflow with hope by the power of the Holy Spirit.

These passages are a powerful confirmation for us that peace is a central tenant of spiritual principle and precept. This doesn't mean we can't get excited at times or experience exuberance, but it does mean that we are not easily riled up and we are not quick to states of hysteria. I don't believe teaching on spiritual warfare was meant to cause such a disruption in our peace. The same Jesus Who encouraged us to be peaceful is the same Jesus Who also pointed out that choosing to follow Him was going to have consequences that were not always going to feel "peaceful" in nature (Matthew 10:35, Luke 12:53). He recognized conflicts would come when we chose to follow Him because not everyone would understand our decision. That does not mean we should avoid peace, nor does it mean we should be void of peace due to others.

It's fine to study spiritual warfare. Proper study of spiritual warfare helps us know how to come against the enemy and how to stand when the enemy comes against us, like a flood (Isaiah 59:19). At the same time, we need to maintain balance to achieve the greatest benefit from all our learning and instruction. Peace is a powerful weapon of the enemy, because it is a movement by which God flows through us. Being chaotic, running around, frenzied and angry all the time is not effective in spiritual warfare. All that does is give the enemy a further foothold to divide and confuse in your situation. Let's never forget that we serve the God of peace, not confusion (1 Corinthians 14:33)!

Achieving peace with others

Philippians 4:4-9 advises:

Rejoice in the Lord always. I will say it again: Rejoice! Let your gentleness be evident to all. The Lord is near. Do not be anxious about anything, but in every situation, by prayer and petition, with thanksgiving, present your requests to God. And the peace of God, which transcends all understanding, will guard your hearts and your minds in Christ Jesus.

Finally, brothers, whatever is true, whatever is noble, whatever is right, whatever is pure, whatever is lovely, whatever is admirable – if anything is excellent or praiseworthy – think about such things. Whatever you have learned or received or heard from me, or seen in me – put it into practice. And the God of peace will be with you.

If we are to achieve peace with others, we need to follow the advice found in the verses above. We need to be people whose conduct is notable for being gentle, calm, and readily relying on the Lord. Rather than being people who pursue the things of the world and try to achieve peace by worldly means that do not, in the long run, work, we need to be people who practice what we preach. If we do right, the God of peace, the source of all our peace, the Prince of Peace (Isaiah 9:6) will be with us. Rather than always trying to fight, we should be people who seek resolution to conflicts.

> **HAPPY HARVEST:** How can studying spiritual warfare help bring you greater peace?

Sometimes that will mean stepping away from some people, no matter how they might be part of our lives. Sometimes it means reconciling, apologizing when we have been wrong and seeking to make things right. Sometimes it means forgiving wrongs done to us, so we can move forward. Sometimes it means stepping out and trying something we've never done before and taking steps towards new things. In all that we do, it does mean that we know the God of peace will be with us, and we take that step of trust in peace to advance spiritually.

Producing more excellent fruit

Where are you when it comes to peace? Where can you do better? Here are some suggestions on ways to produce a more excellent fruit of peace:

- **Research the different peace movements throughout the ages**: Did you know that most of the movements encouraging peace started out in the church? Disturbed by trends of violence and war, pacifism and a belief that Christians should be a peaceful people opposed to war has followed believers through the centuries. Groups such as Anabaptists, Quakers, Mennonites, Amish, and Seventh-day Adventists continue traditions of pacifism, even though we don't hear much about it today. Even though aggression is seen as prime (even among churchgoers), the ideas of the pacifists of every generation are Biblically grounded and a strong centering point for us on matters of peace as we explore its themes in real time.

- **Meditate on Scripture**: "Meditate" is a word used in many ways. In its most minimal definition, to meditate means to think or ponder on something quietly for a period of time. We should all focus on the Scriptures and specifically on God's word spoken to us at different periods in our lives through meditation. Doing such helps bring these things to mind when we are in situations that require them. If we want to be people of peace, we must be people who know and embrace what God says to us. Meditation doesn't have to be long and drawn out, nor does it have to be crazy and strange. Sitting quietly, thinking on passages of Scripture and blessings spoken, and allowing those passages to become alive to us helps instill a sense of peace and serenity surrounding any situation.

- **Finish what you start**: Leaving things unfinished is a common way we experience stress and frustration, especially when we are frantic to finish it. Being punctual, leaving ourselves plenty of time to arrive and complete tasks, completing projects, avoiding procrastination, and keeping our word all contribute to a better sense of peace in our lives.

- **Don't avoid stressful situations…deal with them**: Trying to avoid stress becomes a whole new way to encounter it. Rather than avoiding difficult things, handle them as needed and then move forward to something else. When encountering stress, try techniques of deep breathing, leaving the situation for a little while, re-think ways to handle the situation, be creative, and do whatever it is that you can to resolve a situation rather than letting it drag on and on.

- **Maintain a prayer space**: Keep a place for yourself that is just for prayer. It can be a chair, a corner in a room, a personal altar space, a place in a park or garden, or somewhere more abstract, such as your daily commute to work, your bathroom or bedroom, or kitchen. Your prayer space can be anywhere you are able to focus on prayer and communicate with God without distraction or interruption.

- **Avoid information overload**: I'm all for knowing about current events and things going on in the world, but between nightly news, news channels, the internet, our phones, tablets, and other places that supply an endless stream of current events, it is very easy to get a severe case of information overload. Hearing too many news stories that reflect worldly characteristics and that impress worldly problems becomes a peace disrupting state. It's fine to be informed, but there comes a point in time when it's time to unplug a little bit and stop the "need to know" cycle so much of the time.

- **Monitor your entertainment**: I don't get into the specific "dos" and "don't's" of entertainment because I recognize that people have their own levels of tolerance for things, their own interests, and ability to handle their own programming. That being said, sometimes what we watch, listen to, and absorb through entertainment venues can cause us to feel disquieted within ourselves. Excessive violence and gore can have effects on the mind as well as the body. Sometimes our brains can process unusual interests we have and rewire them into strange or problematic dreams. If you have problems with peace, check on your entertainment sources.

Chapter Five

Patience (Long-Suffering, Forbearance)

THE END OF A MATTER IS BETTER THAN ITS BEGINNING,
AND PATIENCE IS BETTER THAN PRIDE.
DO NOT BE QUICKLY PROVOKED IN YOUR SPIRIT,
FOR ANGER RESIDES IN THE LAP OF FOOLS.
— ECCLESIASTES 7:8-9

Assignments:
- Read James 5:7-12.
- Unplug from all television and social media for twenty-four hours.
- Forgive someone who has repeatedly tried your patience.

*W*ho else is impatient, raise your hand!!!!!!!!!!
What, nobody? Am I the only one?
Oh, come on, you all aren't that holy...are you?

Why do I suddenly have the urge to break into a chorus of *Patience* by Guns N' Roses?

If I am seriously the only one who has ever been really impatient with someone telling a never-ending (boring) story on the phone, having to sit in city rush hour traffic, when ministry seems slow or like things aren't moving real fast, when you are waiting for something to happen, and it just never comes...

I thought that might increase the number of hands in the air.

If the people I've known are any indication, I know very, very few people who exemplify patience by their very nature. Most of the people I've known get bored and want to move on with things far faster than they usually move, and that leads to a state of impatience. Plus, I believe we've all had that one person (ok more like two, or three, or ten) who vexes us. There's just something about them that rubs us the wrong way and causes us to not want to talk or interact with them, let alone doing so in a patient or dignified manner.

For some reason, patience seems to be an area where a lot of people stumble, but no one wants to admit it. The stereotypical church person is stereotyped as very patient, never questioning their situations or ever getting riled or difficult. As a result, people aren't honest about their proclivities toward impatience. We think being impatient is a shameful thing, the worst of the worst, something to admit in a dark closet to a priest sworn to secrecy in the midnight hour.

For a topic we to magnify above all others, there really isn't a whole lot in the Bible about patience. In the entire Bible, a whole of 16 verses graces its pages about patience. I was kind of surprised at this, but that should tell us something about patience: it's something that alludes most people, and is definitely something we all can work toward. If more Bible authors had mastered it or given it the amount of emphasis many do, there would have been far more written on it than there is. While patience is good and important, it's also important not to be deliberately vexing, which the Bible spends a lot more time discussing in one form or another. This is an important balance we don't discuss often enough as we teach on patience without a central balancing point. We over-emphasize patience, but don't tell people that deliberately trying the patience of others is also wrong. If we work on patience and not trying the patience of others, we could have a much better situation in church (not to mention among our families, friends, workplaces, and general society, too!).

Sounds great, doesn't it? Be patient with me (wasn't that clever?) and we'll get to the bottom of this thing we call patience.

> **PRUNING POINTS:** In developing the fruit of the Spirit, why do you think patience is important? How can developing patience help you with other areas of the fruit of the Spirit?

What is patience?

I wish I had some deep answer for everyone as to what patience is. It's not real poetic, it's not real sing-song, it's not real cute, and it's not real clever. Some translations of the Bible translate patience as "forbearance" or "long-suffering," and I think these are great illustrations for us as to what patience is. It is being willing to suffer long, to go the distance, and to tolerate faults and failings within others and ourselves, for a long period of time.

Colossians 1:9-14 says:

For this reason, since the day we heard about you, we have not stopped praying for you. We continually ask God to fill you with the knowledge of His will through all the wisdom and understanding that the Spirit gives, so that you may live a life worthy of the Lord and please Him in every way: bearing fruit in every good work, growing in the knowledge of God, being strengthened with all power according to His glorious might so that you may have great endurance and patience, and giving joyful thanks to the Father, Who has qualified you to share in the inheritance of His holy people in the Kingdom of light. For He has rescued us from the dominion of darkness and brought us into the Kingdom of the Son He loves, in Whom we have redemption, the forgiveness of sins.

- **Patience is persistent and consistent**: Patience is not merely sitting around, waiting for something to happen in your life. It's not, as we would say, happenstance. Patience is steady, persistently and consistently seeking God for the goals and promises He's placed in your life and for the lives of others. Patience clearly prays, consistently stays the course even when it wants to go awry, and steadies itself in a world that wants to rush ahead and miss the point much of the time.

- **Patience brings us to the point where we can bear fruit**: Fruit cultivation is a very involved process. Farmers don't just plant a seed and then watch fruit pop up everywhere. Cultivators of fruit must tend to the process, pay attention to plant development through the process, observe growth patterns, watch for problems in cultivation, meet the nutritional and growing needs of plants, and take them all the way to harvest, where they will transform into something else. This entire process takes patience! It is the same with us and the characteristics God desires to develop within us as pertain to spiritual matters.

- **Patience helps us grow in God**: Growing in God is a process that transforms our entire lives, both inside and out. Just like plant cultivation is a slow process, growing in God can also be on the slow side. It's spoken of as being a walk rather than a plane ride because we don't move fast in it.

Sometimes we run, sometimes we walk backwards, sometimes we trip and stumble, and we don't always get there as quickly as we'd like. At the same time, patience gives us the wisdom to recognize where we need to be, and when. There is no reason to be in a hurry on step 50 if you are only on step two.

- **Patience helps us strengthen and endure**: Patience is a form of endurance, just a bit of a quieter form of it. Rather than making the big fuss that often comes with endurance, patience doesn't require the "fuss." In patience, you go through and remain consistent in everything you need to be doing without having to tell everyone about it, because you have the inner assurance that God is working all things together for your good (Romans 8:28).

- **Patience prepares us for our inheritance**: When people write out wills, they usually write them far in advance, long before anyone will receive the contents therein. It is the same as with us and our inheritance from God. What God has for us is for us, but that doesn't mean we are ready to receive it when we start out...or when we are at the mid-point of our journey. Patience is a preparer, because as we go along in our walk, we come into greater focus for what God has for us and what we are preparing to receive.

- **Patience was part of the salvation process**: We don't often consider that the Old Testament covers at least a 4,000-year period of time. That entire time, God's old covenant people waited for the Messiah, waited for their redemption, went through the motions of

> BUD BREAKS: **Patience**
> #3115 *makrothumia* [mak-roth-oo-mee'-ah]:
> 1) patience, endurance, constancy, steadfastness, perseverance;
> 2) patience, forbearance, longsuffering, slowness in avenging wrongs.

> **FOUNDATIONAL FERTILIZER:** Some years back, we were all set to start work on a church movement in Raleigh. I'd ordered some things to start advertising, the date wasscheduled and the website updated, and then the whole thing fell through because the building we were going to use was led by a minister who wound up going to jail! The church property was raided for evidence and the ministry was forced to close, just weeks before we were supposed to start. Even though this sent me back to the drawing board to find a new property, I was peaceful enough through the trial to realize that patiently waiting to find the right property for this work was better than rushing ahead and creating a mess or getting caught up in someone else's mess because I don't want to wait to receive what God has for us.

the law, falling and failing without much foresight or vision as to when it would all end. When the fullness of time had come (Galatians 4:4-7), God sent forth His Son. As we await the time when we can be with our Savior, when we shall see Him face-to-face (1 Corinthians 13:12), we see the work of salvation as we walk it out with fear and trembling (Philippians 2:12).

The electrical wiring and HVAC system in our spiritual house

We don't consider the electrical and HVAC systems in our homes until they abruptly stop working. The units are there, working via hundreds of networks, signals, and receptors, all delivering the lighting, cooling, and heat we need, as we need them. As we build the house, they are installed after foundational aspects of the property but are just as important to creating stable and essential living conditions for those who will dwell in the residence.

Patience operates the same way. We don't know patience isn't present until it's clearly not. Then, the hundreds of little choices, circumstances, situations, and issues we face every day quickly contribute to our dwindling patience. It stabilizes our lives, is there when we need and require it, and makes sure that every time we want to do so something, God's light helps us get through difficult situations by comforting us with the Holy Spirit (John 14:26, John

16:7-8). Patience is essential to conducting the presence of God in our lives in just the way we need it.

Peace and patience

Patience is that it is connected to a lot of things, many more than we might like to admit. The reason patience isn't the world's most comfortably defined virtue is for this reason: to achieve patience, we have to have balance and achieve balance in many different areas of our lives. That's why patience is mentioned toward the middle of the fruit of the Spirit, not at the beginning or the end. It is at the very center of developing all these other characteristics and virtues, because it gives us the ability to really make something of all of them. Patience doesn't just come about because we want it to, or because we're born like that. Even people who seem to wait well most likely have some area of their lives where they are impatient, ready to give up, frustrated, or hope to avenge a wrong done to them.

Perhaps most clearly, patience and peace are deeply connected. We can't have patience if we are not peaceful as people. If we are disquieted within, then we will be disquieted without. We will then be impatient and dissatisfied with our lives. As peace is God moving within us, patience is the result of that. Rather than being in a rush to do this or that or come here or go there, patience displays constant hope and promise that God will do what He promised in His timing rather than ours. Patience is adjusting to God's timing in life without losing sight of the things we need to continue to do while we trust in Him.

All things together for your good

There's an oft-quoted Bible verse that intricately relates to patience, but actually never mentions the word "patience." The chapter itself talks a lot about life in the Spirit, and about the things that are to come that we do not yet see with our eyes but know by faith. This passage is Romans 8:18-30:

I consider that our present sufferings are not worth comparing with the glory that will be revealed in us. The creation awaits in eager expectation for the children of God to be revealed. For the creation was subjected to frustration, not by its own choice, but by the will of the One Who subjected it, in hope that the creation itself will be liberated from its bondage to decay and brought into the freedom and glory of the children of God.

We know that the whole creation has been groaning as in the pains of childbirth right up to the present time. Not only so, but we ourselves, who have the firstfruits of the Spirit, groan inwardly as we wait eagerly for our adoption to sonship, the redemption of our bodies. For in this hope we were saved. But hope that is seen is no hope at all. Who hopes for what they already have? But if we hope for what we do not yet have, we wait for it patiently.

In the same way, the Spirit helps us in our weakness. We do not know what we ought to pray for, but the Spirit Himself intercedes for us through wordless groans. And He Who searches our hearts knows the mind of the Spirit, because the Spirit intercedes for God's people in accordance with the will of God.

> **POWER POLLINATION:** Has God told you to pray or believe with someone and you have stopped praying and believing out of frustration? God is long-suffering with all of us. Next time you want to give up on someone God has told you to pray and believe with and for, remember how difficult it must have been for someone who was assigned to intercede for and pray for and with you, too!

And we know that in all things God works for the good of those who love Him, who have been called according to His purpose. For those God foreknew He also predestined to be conformed to the likeness of His Son, that He might be the firstborn among many brothers and sisters. And those He predestined, He also called; those He called, He also justified; those He justified, He also glorified.

The truth about patience is found right here, present in these passages that we quote over and over again to mean everything, but the patience required for our spiritual walk. I have quoted an extensive part of Romans 8 along with the popular verses because these additional passages prove to us how our walk with God is frequently difficult. Even though we hear a lot about money and easy lives, these aren't things God promises us. What God does tell us here is that we must maintain our walk of faith through patience, as we believe and trust for the plan of God to continue to unfold in His timing.

This passage of Scripture doesn't prove that people are predestined, but that the plan of God is predestined by a heavenly Father Who knows the end from the beginning and already knows who will receive and reject His grace. As we make our choices accordingly, we groan at times along with creation, because we have not yet received nor seen the fullness of our redemption. We believe for it, we know it is coming, but the "in the meantime" periods of life are often difficult to endure and challenging to navigate.

Our blessing of endurance is the work of the Spirit in our lives, interceding and moving on our behalf toward all that we need. The Spirit helps push us through our weaknesses, guides us through His own intercessions and our own prayers, and yes, trusts that what God works for us is for our good, as we follow what He has called us to do. This whole spiritual walk is all a big, long walk of patience!

Attributes of patience

So what does patience look like? Is it a nice, quiet old woman on the bus who isn't in a hurry? What is God trying to teach us through patience? What we learn about patience may surprise us, because in patience we are learning about the heart of God, how He views each one of us, and how He forebears with each and every one of us through our own walk of faith.

James 5:7-9 says:

Be patient, then, brothers and sisters, until the Lord's coming. See how the farmer waits for the land to yield its valuable crop, patiently waiting for the autumn and spring rains. You too, be patient and stand firm, because the Lord's coming is near. Don't grumble against each other, brothers and sisters, or you will be judged. The Judge is standing at the door!

Many people talk about patience as the way we wait or how we handle a state of waiting. It is true that patience does relate to how well we can wait, but patience isn't just about waiting. It's about a general attitude toward life, as well as a comprehensive way of life. Patient people stand firm when others fall apart and make it a point to investigate all things that help them to stand firm.

Patience comes with a certain level of understanding. The farmer can is patient as he awaits the time when his crops are ready because he understands – he knows how – the crops function and operate. He recognizes the times and the seasons, and he knows what needs to be done when it needs to be done. We could say that patience is a way of handling life and handling it with confidence. If we know the different stages and trust what comes next, it helps us to be more patient with the things that come along in life.

This understanding helps us to refrain from constant grumbling and bickering with others. It's easy to judge things on the surface and never consider things that might go on that you don't know about. Instead of disrupting your world and the world of others…maybe it's better to step back and think about what might be going on in that other person's life…and let an offense pass.

James 5:10-12:

Brothers and sisters, as an example of patience in the face of suffering, take the prophets who spoke in the Name of the Lord. As you know, we count as blessed those who have persevered. You have heard of Job's perseverance and have seen what the Lord finally brought about. The Lord is full of compassion and mercy.

Above all, my brothers and sisters, do not swear – not by heaven or by earth or by anything else. All you need to say is a simple "Yes" or "No." Otherwise you will be condemned.

Ahhh…Job. I wondered when he was going to come up. Coming up in church, we used to talk about the "patience of Job." People used Job as an example of patience and waiting well, and all that sort of stuff. I think we need to look at Job a little more carefully, though, to reveal something important: Job was not "patient" according to our definitions assigned to patience. In fact, if we assess Job's behavior along the lines of "waiting well," Job was rather impatient. This must mean if Job was considered "enduring" in the eyes of God, it is our definition of patience that needs a shift!

> **PRUNING POINTS:** Job had a long talk with God about the mysteries of wisdom and the wonder of creation in connection with his intense period of suffering. Rather than asking God to take away your suffering, how can you look at your personal periods of trial, discuss them with God, and learn from them?

All things considered, I don't think we are fair with Job today, especially in judging ourselves. We are quick to brand him as proud or self-righteous, when that isn't what the Bible says about him (Job 1:1-8). Job was a good man, an honest man, who was selected for the "ultimate test" by Satan, because the enemy thought he could get Job to break. Job endured each trial, each thing Satan threw his way, each problem he had through that period in his life, and despite all of it, he didn't give up on God. He whined sometimes, he complained, but all in all, Job had a long discussion with God that proved it's not that we have the wrong answers, but that we are asking the wrong questions.

There's a little bit of Job in every believer. We go through things, the enemy comes against us, and we are put in situations where we must be long-suffering. We go through difficult conditions for a long time, resisting the temptation to give up on God or change our course. If anything, we can learn a lot from Job about patience and what it means to be patient. Patience doesn't mean we don't seek out explanation or ask questions when things happen. It doesn't mean that we don't cry out to God in a difficult situation. Patience means we stick with God no matter what is going on, and we keep attending to His matters, no matter how hard the enemy or others make it for us.

In keeping with the parallel to Job, the prophets of old also dealt with incredible odds, especially from other people. This did not deter them from their appointed work and their appointed message. They had to be long-suffering (enduring, encountering, putting up) with the people whom they were sent to deliver God's message. That didn't mean they never spoke up about what people were doing wrong, and it certainly never meant they didn't cry out to God or experience extreme frustration over the things that they had to deal with. It simply meant that they endured…and got through it…and still trusted God, no matter how hard it was.

Patient is love…

We looked at 1 Corinthians 13:4 in an earlier chapter:

Love is patient, love is kind…

As was pointed out in chapter 2, we don't think about what "love" really is. In looking at the attributes of love, we learned that love is patient. The reverse of this is patience is love. Whenever we walk in patience, extending it to someone else, we are showing someone that we love them. When we walk in patience, we also show God that we love Him enough to obey Him, even when it's hard.

The bottom line of patience is that it is hard. The times that require it most are the times that require us to exemplify the love of God the most. This is usually when we want to do it the least. If we are to be people that go through, and go through well, we need to remember in all things that patience is, truly, a reflection of our love.

Patience and contention

Patience and contention aren't two things we hear about often in the same sentence. People who are patient aren't particularly seen as contentious, and vice-versa. The truth, however, is that patience and contention need to be discussed together. Too often, we teach the answer to contention is infinite patience. We're told to give into the demands and requests of contentious people. We also teach that contentious people may be put in our lives to help us develop more patience. I don't believe this is necessarily true, because the basis of this understanding is grounded in the belief that patience is all about pacifying other people who feed off others by being difficult.

Different translations of the Bible translate the word "contention" or "contentious" differently, including "self-seeking" (New International Version), "selfishly ambitious" (New American Standard Bible), "factious" (American Standard Version) and "self-willed" (Weymouth New Testament). It is obvious the type of person discussed here is someone who is deliberately willful, trying to get attention and control by their behavior. The way contentious people operate is by irritating, arguing, and frustrating other people.

Proverbs 21:19:

It is better to dwell in the wilderness, than with a contentious and an angry woman. (KJV)

Proverbs 26:21:

As coals are to burning coals, and wood to fire; so is a contentious man to kindle strife. (KJV)

Proverbs 27:15:

A continual dropping in a very rainy day and a contentious woman are alike. (KJV)

Romans 2:8:

But unto them that are contentious, and do not obey the truth, but obey unrighteousness, indignation and wrath… (KJV)

Contention is mentioned nowhere in the Bible as a virtuous or positive characteristic. It is not desirable, and clearly applies across the board for all people alike. Such behavior is not appropriate, especially for the believer. There is no good or justifiable reason to simply vex and irritate others. In response to such, frustration and annoyance are completely rational and understandable. Frustration from contention reminds us of what can happen when we frustrate the grace of God in our lives.

Galatians 2:16-21:

Know that a person is not justified by the works of the law, but by faith in Jesus Christ. So we, too, have put our faith in Christ Jesus that we may be justified by faith in Christ and not by the works of the law, because by the works of the law no one will be justified.

"But if, in seeking to be justified in Christ, we Jews find ourselves among the sinners, doesn't that mean that Christ promotes sin? Absolutely not! If I rebuild what I destroyed, then I really would be a lawbreaker.

"For through the law I died to the law so that I might live for God. I have been crucified with Christ and I no longer live, but Christ lives in me. The life I now live in the body, I live by faith in the Son of God, Who loved me and gave Himself for me. I do not set aside the grace of God, for if righteousness could be gained through the law, Christ died for nothing!"

This passage is of eternal importance and modern relevance, just as it was in days gone by, for a lot of reasons. Every one of us needs the reminder that we are not saved by ourselves, nor are we saved by the works of the law, our ideas about the law, or by our judgments of other people (or our own re-created concepts therein). All throughout history, people have attempted to operate via their own means of righteousness. They do this by creating their own law, or more than likely, their own version of the law. No matter what tower we build to ourselves in order to keep ourselves sheltered, we create a means by which we do not have to confront our own sins. If we simply do not associate with certain people out of a sense of self-righteousness, we create our own law. If we hold ourselves above other people because we consider ourselves to be superior, we create our own law. If we are not doing what God has asked of us and calling that "grace," we create our own law.

In terms of contentious people, we constantly deal with others who think they "know best" about whatever they discuss. Our world is full of "casual scholars," those who think they read a few paragraphs of something online or watched a few YouTube videos and now they know more than everyone else. This has caused contention to soar sky-high and has left us square in the middle of a world full of extremes. We see one end of "dos and don'ts," and another extreme of disobedience, no matter what they may claim. Both are equally frustrating to God and are frustrations of His grace to us. Grace has not been given to us as an excuse to disobey what God says, nor is it an excuse to just modify our relationship with Him to suit our own personal need to be self-righteous and personally glorified. As with all things in the Father, God calls us to seek the balance - the middle ground - between these two excessive extremes. When we find balance, we are grounded in a place that ceases to frustrate His grace.

Just as I (or any individual dealing with a contentious person) see my time as valuable and feel disrespect when it is dishonored, so too does God see His grace as a valuable and precious thing. When we dishonor the grace He has freely given to us, God feels dishonored. We focus a lot on character development away from impatience and intolerance, but we often don't flip the coin and look at the reverse. Sometimes people are as patient as they have within them to be, and people continue to grate on that. Sometimes people lash out or say things that perhaps they shouldn't, but sometimes they are provoked. In this instance, the goodness they have has been frustrated - and the result is a sense of anger. It is not a vain anger, but a righteous one - one that in an honest setting should cause all to step back and look at themselves.

> **FOUNDATIONAL FERTILIZER:** Most of us have, at one point in time or another, played games via social media online. Did you ever notice now many of those games are agriculturally themed? There is a reason for that! Agricultural games bring with them a sense of patience and discipline required to master its different levels. Every time we play a game like this, and we don't walk away or use the "cheats" that are built into the game to help us achieve the different levels, we are developing patience!

We don't like to think of God as angry or displeased. We certainly don't like to think of ourselves as having the ability to "frustrate" God's grace. We want to think it's not possible to frustrate it, simply because it's from God - but the Bible doesn't give us that perspective. Modern-day ministries tend to emphasize certain attributes of God that are appealing to people - and, in turn, advocate these attributes in people, which often equates to a manipulative form of people-pleasing. This turns, over time, into a source of control for people, who think the witchcraft they work is some sort of mainstream for "faith." I call it the "First Church of Make Nice." Many believe Jesus came to earth to "Make Nice" with humanity and now God "Makes Nice" with us. In such ridiculous theory, this also means that we should "Make Nice" with each other. It's not supposed to matter if they are frustrating not just us, but God, as well. It doesn't matter how annoying or frustrating someone is - we're supposed to pretend we are all right with how they behave. This is considered character-building. No, what it is, is dishonest. I agree that sometimes we need to be understanding, but sometimes we need to just tell people, with a true spirit of love and honesty, that their behavior is unacceptable. Grace does not exist so we can be endlessly needy or annoying, nor does it exist so we can be self-righteous and pompous with one another.

We want to hear about the mercy, grace, and patience of God, but we don't want to hear about the flip side, which is our own doing: frustrating the grace of God. God is loving, merciful, and patient, but the Bible specifically commands us not to frustrate the grace of God. In other words, we have the same commandment from the beginning: be obedient. God still doesn't like self-righteousness. He still does not like disobedience. His work and grace still stand, but we are still called to cooperate with the work He does within us. In the end, the choice remains ours as to whether we frustrate God's grace. I write this we can all take a good, long look at ourselves and the things we must work out to move to the place He has for us. How are we out of balance in our lives? How is that frustrating God's grace? How are we, as a type, frustrating others with our out-of-balance approach? How can we be better prepared for what God is asking us to do?

Our personal frustration is a type, a shadow, and reminder of what God experiences with each of us when we frustrate His grace. Next time you have this experience, step back and think about the work God wants to do within you...and take the steps to do it. Instead of seeing it as an opportunity to change your character, let it cause you to examine ways that you can be frustrating to God, or frustrating to others, and do what you can to change those characteristics within yourself. Give them to God and turn closer to Him and away from contentious, vexing behavior. Getting frustrated doesn't mean one is not patient; it simply means something is vexing them…and vexing others is not a part of God's Kingdom.

Patience and maturity

The last thing we are going to look at in-depth as pertains to patience is patience and its role in maturity. Children are impatient by nature, because they have not learned how to persevere through life yet. This is why things such as teaching children to wait their turn, to stick with projects and other things they desire to pursue and encouraging them to do their best even with subjects they don't like or find challenging are so important. Patience is something we develop deeper as we get older (if we don't desire to be contentious, that is) and move toward better and greater things for us.

People who are immature in their faith do not model patience. They want to give up when things get too difficult, and they have a hard time accepting others as they are. They dislike having to disconnect and focus on God, and have trouble being still and waiting on God's timing in their lives.

It is God's desire that, through patience, we can gain a better understanding of the work God is doing within every one of us. In speaking on the work of patience in his own life, the Apostle Paul said the following in 1 Timothy 1:15-16:

> **HAPPY HARVEST:** How have you grown in patience since starting this study on the fruit of the Spirit?

Here is a trustworthy saying that deserves full acceptance: Christ Jesus came into the world to save sinners — of whom I am the worst. But for that very reason I was shown mercy so that in me, the worst of sinners, Christ Jesus might display His immense patience as an example for those who would believe in Him and receive eternal life.

Simply put, every one of us is called to grow up, mature, and develop a deeper understanding of the way God operates through us. No matter how difficult, contentious, willful, proud, or sinful we can be, God can do a work through us if we are willing to trust Him enough to let Him do that work. We can see God's unlimited patience in the fact that, while we have not always done things that were pleasing to Him, we are able to say He has not destroyed us and is willing to give us the chance to do what we should do. Now, in maturity, we offer that same offer to other people through the fruit of patience.

Producing more excellent fruit

Where are you when it comes to patience? Where can you do better? Here are some suggestions on ways to produce a more excellent fruit of patience:

- **Ask some bigger life questions**: Earlier we talked about the fact that asking too many "big" life questions can cause one to lose their joy, because we will never figure out the answers to all the deep questions in our lifetime. Not asking them enough, however, can cause us to be out of balance in other areas of life. Thinking about some of the bigger things – like wisdom, life, and the promises of eternity – keep us grounded and humble. They also help us realize that in the scope of the world, we aren't the biggest thing around. These things help to keep us patient.

- **Learn how to unplug**: I love that I can keep in contact with people at the click of a button or an app on the phone but making our interactions so easy and so anonymous has led to a whole new breed of contentious people. It's easy to spend so much time in the virtual world that we start taking on the nature of contention ourselves. Take some time and unplug, if for no other reason, to get away from the contention bred through internet ignorance, hostility, and anger. Don't let the world's high tech methods cause you to feel contentious yourself.

- **Learn how to forgive**: Another attribute that belongs to love, patience accepts people the way they are and recognizes if they want to have others in their lives, they will have to forebear some characteristics deemed unpleasant. Forgiveness is in order more times than not! Extending forgiveness is a beautiful thing when trying to master the fine characteristic of patience.

- **Sing some of the old church hymns in your worship times**: As much as I love modern worship, I can't deny there is something special about the church songs that people have sang, throughout generations, echoing the perseverance of the saints in every age. We need to remember these songs and sing them ourselves, even on occasion, because they require discipline and patience to sing! Most are written in harmonic arrangements, have multiple verses that make it impossible to memorize all the words, and dictate that when singing them, we focus on what we are doing. Let those songs and those words transport you to a more patient reality as you can hear salvation's promise in every note.

- **Cook a meal from scratch**: Some people really like cooking, and some people do not. As one who never cared for scratch cooking when I was younger, I've come to appreciate its still and art while also embracing shortcuts here and there. Either way, cooking from scratch takes patience as the result of careful planning, because it takes time to prepare the food for cooking and then waiting during the cooking process.

- **Spend some time with children or the elderly**: If you are a part of a ministry that has a children's church, nursery, children's ministry, or outreach to the elderly, get involved and learn about how vital and important it is to spend time with people who are at points in their lives that demand patient interaction.

- **Take up a game or craft that involves extensive skill**: Whether it's sewing, quilting, knitting, cooking, crossword puzzles, crocheting, woodworking, card games, or something else, there are many different things that cause us to think and work hard in order to see good results. Pick something out that has interested you for awhile...and develop the fruit of patience!

Chapter Six

Kindness

"But show me unfailing kindness like the Lord's kindness
as long as I live, so that I may not be killed,
and do not ever cut off your kindness from my family –
not even when the Lord has cut off every one of David's
enemies from the face of the earth."

So Jonathan made a covenant with the house of David, saying,
"May the Lord call David's enemies to account." And
Jonathan had David reaffirm his oath out of love
for him, because he loved him as he loved himself.
– 1 Samuel 20:14-17

Assignments:
- Read 2 Corinthians 6:3-13.
- Lend or give away a copy of your favorite spiritual book to a family member or friend.
- Write a thank-you note to a leader or mentor who has helped you in your life, either past or present.

Little kids are often shown short videos on the values of "kindness." We tell children, as we were told, that it's good to be kind to each other. They sing songs about it, recite verses about it, talk about it in school, and think about ways they can be kind to one another. They should share toys, not run with scissors (or other sharp objects), pick up after themselves, and include others in group games.

It's hard to believe watching news clips that anyone ever received this sort of instruction. We hear horror stories of students who are mercilessly teased, bullied, treated unfairly, and cruelly humiliated, some to the point of suicide. Then we watch so-called adults try to bully and intimidate others through fits of road rage, online on social networking sites over disagreements of opinion, and virulently fighting and antagonizing each other. None of these behaviors reflect those practices we learned as children: sharing, thinking of others, wanting the best for everyone, and behaving in a dignified way as we interact with other people.

I think the larger world recognizes we have a kindness problem, or maybe we should say an unkindness problem. For many years, talk show hosts and other celebrities have advocated the average person start doing "random acts of kindness" for others (buying a cup of coffee, paying for a drive-through order, etc.) you don't know. Occasionally we see commercials advocating kindness and appreciation for others, strong encouragements hoping people will do things that are nice and considerate for one another. The hope is that maybe because of something people see, it will make us be better people.

The problem with suggestion and even imitation is that we

can't force others to become decent human beings. We can't make people think of others, do nice things for them, help others out when they are in need, or speak nicely and with forethought to their neighbors. It's great to think a famous person's commercial campaign will make people be kind, but it isn't that simple. Kindness is something that must be developed within each one of us, something that we make a conscientious effort to engage in and to do as we go throughout our days. In kindness, we don't just think about other people, we reach out and do things for them. We take our actions and match them with the thoughts, the *agape* love we should all have, and make sure that we are reaching out in the way God would have us to do, one person at a time.

Kindness is something we can benefit from exploring for ourselves in a fuller sense. In kindness, we get out of our own small, insular worlds and start realizing there is so much more out there for us to do, explore, and yes, souls to reach as we walk through our life of faith this side of heaven.

What is kindness?

Perhaps kindness could be described as love in action. Kindness is what we do, an expression of our love for God and for others. It is also God's expressions of love to us, manifest in all the different ways that He can and does impact our lives. No matter how you spin it, think about it, regard it, or handle it, kindness is clearly an action. We can't be kind and keep it to

> BUD BREAKS:
> **Kindness** *#5544 chrestotes* {khray-stot'-ace}: 1) moral goodness, integrity; 2) benignity, kindness.

ourselves, because it just doesn't work like that. If we are to be people who both receive and give kindness, we must be doing things.

Kindness is not without its purpose. We don't just do kind things to make ourselves feel good or to make us look good on a resume or project summary. Kindness is about some very deep spiritual principles that help lead us and others to the Lord. As it points out in Romans 2:1-11:

You, therefore, have no excuse, you who pass judgment on someone else, for at whatever point you judge another, you are condemning yourself, because you who pass judgment do the same things. Now we know that God's judgment against those who do such things is based on truth. So when you, a mere human being, pass judgment on them and yet do the same things, do you think you will escape God's judgment? Or do you show contempt for the riches of His kindness, forbearance and patience, not realizing that God's kindness is intended to lead you to repentance?

But because of your stubbornness and your unrepentant heart, you are storing up wrath against yourself for the day of God's wrath, when His righteous judgment will be revealed. God "will repay each person according to what they has done." To those who by persistence in doing good seek glory, honor, and immortality, He will give eternal life. But for those who are self-seeking and who reject the truth and follow evil, there will be wrath and anger. There will be trouble and distress for every human being who does evil: first for the Jew, then for the Gentile; but glory, honor, and peace for everyone who does good: first for the Jew, then for the Gentile. For God does not show favoritism.

- **Kindness does not pass judgment**: Judgment is a hot-button topic in both today's church and the world, as well. The world often throws around a handful of Bible verses in the face of staunch churchgoers who seem judgmental would have us think the world knows more of the Bible than the church! The truth, however, isn't quite that simple. While yes, the world is right that church folk can be judgmental, the world can be as judgmental as the church. Judgment isn't a religious issue; it's a human one. Attempting to point fingers elsewhere doesn't nullify our personal judgments.

  No matter how hard we might try to justify judgments (including our personal reasoning, using Scriptures, or being openly spiteful), we can't call ourselves "kind" and "judgmental" at the same time. If we are truly walking in kindness, we are not going to pick at others and make them feel as if they are being judged.

- **Kindness is based in truth:** If God is kind and He leads us to all truth, then kindness is not just love in action, it's also truth in action. As believers, we can try to talk to people about truth as a recitation of our doctrinal beliefs all day long. We can make truth sound like dry words on a book's page, complicated and unobtainable, for years on end. There is no end to the study of "truth" in a scholarly or textual context. As much as I love the study of truth and the discussion of it as an entity, such a scholarly pursuit isn't for everyone. Brilliant words won't change this world. We can either tell people about truth, or we can show them. Kindness is showing them.

- **Kindness embodies tolerance and patience:** Now we get to two of our favorite things! It's amazing how quick Christians are to speak of their intolerances: they dislike this, they dislike that, they have no tolerance for this, they won't tolerate that. The Bible clearly tells us that kindness is akin to tolerance, which is basically a form of forbearance or long-suffering. It's important to show such when you don't necessarily agree with someone else's feelings, habits, beliefs, or specifications of the dreaded "lifestyle" label. Along with tolerance comes patience. Rather than trying to jump in and change people, we must step back and allow God to work within others, supporting them along their journey.

- **Kindness leads us toward repentance:** The purpose of kindness is not to enable wrongdoing. God isn't kind to us because He wants wickedness to continue. He is kind to us because in His kindness, He leads us to a place of repentance. Every single one of us can tell a story about how God displayed kindness and mercy when we deserved it least and how. In hindsight, that brought us to a place of realization; we knew we needed to turn ourselves around. Kindness shows us that God cares and that He desires us to be close to Him.

- **Kindness is not stubborn, nor unrepentant**: Now is the time for a long, silent pause as we consider ourselves in lieu of this realization. Most of us, whether we admit it or not, are stubborn in some ways. What we don't consider is that stubbornness is self-willed. It is wanting one's own way and being unwilling to compromise, no matter how much evidence is proven to the contrary. It's fine to hold your ground when God has given you a vision and the enemy attacks it, but it is not fine to be stubborn just to be stubborn. Kindness is also not unrepentant, meaning that if you commit a wrong against someone else or do something otherwise against God, you repent and ask for forgiveness rather than insisting you were fine in your actions.

- **Kindness is "doing good"**: Kindness doesn't just think or hope good things will happen. It doesn't "wish people well" without doing something for them. Kindness isn't a good thought; it's a good action.

- **Kindness is not evil**: If you're repaying evil for evil or living your life around principles of retaliation and hatred, you are not living in kindness.

- **Kindness does not show favoritism**: Perhaps the most important precept of kindness: it doesn't play favorites. We like to play favorites at church, hang out with people we like and espouse friends who share our values and ideals. It's fine to have friends, it's even fine to hang out with people, but it's not fine to constantly exclude others, because this equates to favoritism. Kindness is bestowed upon all who receive it.

> **POWER POLLINATION**: Think of a list of three ways to be kind to three different people and go do those things for them.

The insulation of our spiritual house

I compare kindness to insulation because insulation works to keep out cold and keep in warmth. This is what kindness does for our spiritual lives: it keeps out the enemy's cold and keeps in God's warmth. One of the biggest complaints I hear Christians in general from both believers and non-believers alike is that people who attend church seem "cold" or "unwelcoming." If we, as a church, were truly dwelling in kindness, these perceptions would not be.

Kindness brings an air of warmth and fellowship to any sort of gathering, focusing on the tasks of doing good for others and welcoming other people into fellowship. These are prime and essential aspects of what our faith is about. Kindness is something people can see, feel, perceive, and above all, experience. Insulation may not be the most cosmetic aspect of a house, but it is certainly one of the most important in making sure a house is kept at the right temperature, so its inhabitants remain comfortable. Kindness may not be the easiest aspect of a person's walk with God. It might not always be the most "cosmetic" or perfect-looking to others, but it is certainly essential to make sure that God's house is welcoming and open to any and all who seek Him in a deeper way.

Kindness is what we do

We like the idea of kindness as a fairy-tale: the pretty fairy-lady comes in and sprinkles us all with magical dust, and we become kind. The truth about kindness is a lot rawer than that. Throughout our lives, we are confronted with circumstances by which we can choose to be kind, or we can choose to behave in an ugly way. Many people assume kindness to be something that comes along and makes us feel fuzzy in different circumstances, but this cannot be further from the truth. If anything, kindness is often most required and efficacious in circumstances where it is lacking or where it doesn't conclude with a deep, warm, fuzzy moment.

We love the story of Ruth because we think it was a storybook romance, the perfect inclusion for every wanting woman…when nothing could be further from the truth. The book of Ruth is a story of survival, of Jew and Gentile coming together in the kinsman-redeemer, and ultimately, of how one woman's kindness brought her and her mother-in-law into a place of destiny.

Ruth 1:1-14:

In the days when the judges ruled, there was a famine in the land. So a man from Bethlehem in Judah, together with his wife and two sons, went to live for a while in the country of Moab. The man's name was Elimelek, his wife's name was Naomi, and the names of his two sons were Mahlon and Kilion. They were Ephrathites from Bethlehem, Judah. And they went to Moab and lived there.

Now Elimelech, Naomi's husband, died, and she was left with her two sons. They married Moabite women, one named Orpah and the other Ruth. After they had lived there about ten years, both Mahlon and Kilion also died, and Naomi was left without her two sons and her husband.

When Naomi heard in Moab that the LORD had come to the aid of His people by providing food for them, she and her daughters-in-law prepared to return home from there. With her two daughters-in-law she left the place where she had been living and set out on the road that would take them back to the land of Judah.

Then Naomi said to her two daughters-in-law, "Go back, each of you, to your mother's home. May the LORD show kindness to you, as you have shown to your dead husbands and to me. May the LORD grant that each of you will find rest in the home of another husband."

Then she kissed them goodbye and they wept aloud and said to her, "We will go back with you to your people."

But Naomi said, "Return home, my daughters. Why would you come with me? Am I going to have any more sons, who could become your husbands? Return home, my daughters; I am too old to have another husband. Even if I thought there was still hope for me – even if I had a husband tonight and then gave birth to sons – would you wait until they grew up? Would you remain unmarried for them? No, my daughters. It is more bitter for me than for you, because the LORD's hand has turned against me!"

At this they wept aloud again. Then Orpah kissed her mother-in-law goodbye, but Ruth clung to her.

The emotional and mental climate of the family, reduced from six to three members, was not good. All of them incurred severe loss. For Naomi, the matriarch, the loss was deep and unbearable. Both Orpah and Ruth stuck around for awhile, showing kindness to Naomi. They mourned their husbands, they honored the dead according to the required traditions, and even beyond that, they stayed around to help Naomi through her grieving process. The Bible doesn't tell us how long it was from the time the men died until the time when the book of Ruth begins. However long it had been, Naomi received kindness from both of her daughters-in-law. They grieved together, lived together, and supported one another. To summarize this point of the story, Naomi felt their support and kindness toward her reached their pinnacle, and it was time for her to consider their needs and send them home. The kindness of these two women, no matter how hard things might have been, didn't encourage Naomi enough. Nothing could break through her sadness and grief to help her experience life. Despite the kindness she was shown, Naomi still felt her life was over.

Sometimes our kindness doesn't "show up and show out" like we'd hope it would. Naomi is an example of this. These two women dedicated themselves and, at that point, their lives to helping their mother-in-law survive, but she still felt hopeless. It's not a wonder that, given the chance to go, Orpah took the opportunity. I am sure she had her own mourning to resolve that went unattended as she tried too hard to help her mother and sister-in-law through kindness. She probably felt lost, like her kindness was a waste, of none effect. Naomi didn't feel any better and Orpah's situation, in the natural realm, looked bleak.

It's easy to judge Orpah. Many people who read Ruth do judge her, feeling she abandoned Naomi and Ruth. But if we are honest with ourselves, we can all identify with her. Some of us have given of kindness until it's given out and we are tired. Orpah received Naomi's kindness in her release to return home to her own people, to have her own life.

Ruth, however, had a different assignment designated for her kindness. It was her choice to remain with Naomi.

Ruth 1:15-22:

"Look," said Naomi, "your sister-in-law is going back to her people and her gods. Go back with her."

But Ruth replied, "Don't urge me to leave you or to turn back from you. Where you go I will go, and where you stay I will stay. Your people will be my people and your God my God. Where you die I will die, and there I will be buried. May the LORD deal with me, be it ever so severely, if even death separates you and me." When Naomi realized that Ruth was determined to go with her, she stopped urging her.

So the two women went on until they came to Bethlehem. When they arrived in Bethlehem, the whole town was stirred because of them, and the women exclaimed, "Can this be Naomi?"

"Don't call me Naomi," she told them. "Call me Mara, because the Almighty has made my life very bitter. I went away full, but the LORD has brought me back empty. Why call me Naomi? The LORD has afflicted me; the Almighty has brought misfortune upon me."

So Naomi returned from Moab accompanied by Ruth the Moabite, her daughter-in-law, arriving in Bethlehem as the barley harvest was beginning.

> **FOUNDATIONAL FERTILIZER:** At one time, I put a lot of time into certain people, hoping they would return my "kindness" and help with the ministry. Time after time, people did not respond to what I did, and I would get angry with them. One day, God asked me, "Are you doing this so they will like you, or because I told you to do it?" Why are you kind? Check your motives!

A thorough review of the above verses reveal what Ruth encountered as she extended kindness to Naomi. It's great to portray Ruth as an eternally patient woman, but Ruth was still a human being, in a very difficult circumstance. As a woman who spent over five years as a widow caring for an older parent, I know being kind to Naomi wasn't always easy for Ruth. She had to handle her own emotions, feelings, thoughts, and personal bitterness over her situation while still considering Naomi and her needs. Circumstances of life tend to change people, and Naomi changed from a pleasant woman into a bitter, angry woman, suffering through unimaginable loss. Coupled with her grief, she felt as if she no longer had any life or purpose. She probably wasn't a lot of fun to be around. At times, it must have felt like a real drag to hang around a woman who was ready to up and die for lack of meaning in her life.

But Ruth didn't give up on Naomi, and she didn't give up on kindness. Despite the difficulties she might have encountered as she tried to reach Naomi in a kind way, Ruth continued. Her story of being willing to move, work in hard labor in the fields, listen to Naomi's advice, and follow it until the end of walking into a place of destiny had its difficult points. Ultimately, Ruth's work shows us that kindness can bring about change, even in the most difficult circumstances. It may not always be immediate, and we might have to put some effort into it, but kindness brings us to a place where God not only works in the lives of others…He also works in ours.

Attributes of kindness

Kindness has a definitive look. It's not pretending to pacify someone in the hopes you can have your turn next. It's not making pleasantries or being fake with other people. If we truly want to be kind, we need to see kindness for what it truly is.

2 Corinthians 6:3-10:

We put no stumbling block in anyone's path, so that our ministry will not be discredited. Rather, as servants of God we commend ourselves in every way: in great endurance; in troubles, hardships and distresses; in beatings, imprisonments and riots; in hard work, sleepless nights and hunger; in purity, understanding, patience and kindness; in the Holy Spirit and in sincere love; in truthful speech and in the power of God; with weapons of righteousness in the right hand and in the left; through glory and dishonor, bad report and good report; genuine, yet regarded as impostors; known, yet regarded as unknown; dying, and yet we live on; beaten, and yet not killed; sorrowful, yet always rejoicing; poor, yet making many rich; having nothing, and yet possessing everything.

It might not seem, at least on the surface, that this passage is about kindness. If we examine it a little deeper, it's absolutely about kindness – about the work of ministry from the perspective of its necessary sacrifice and spiritual goodness. Through its words, we see another example of kindness exemplified in difficult and trying circumstances.

When we think of kindness, we often mistake it for manipulation through action. At other times, we might think it's a form of enabling or saying that behavior is acceptable when it's not. If there's anything we can learn from the Apostle Paul's words, it's that kindness has a purpose, but it's not to manipulate or enable. People don't need permission, nor approval, to do much of what they do. People do what they are going to do no matter what we do or say to them. Kindness isn't enabling other people to do wrong. Instead, it pushes them in the direction to do right, by extending a sense of love toward them. Kindness extends a hand of understanding, removing the stumbling blocks often placed in people's paths to make them deliberately encounter troubles. Let's pause for a moment and think about that. How often do we deliberately allow people to stumble, instead of doing something to help them out? Kindness doesn't do this! It doesn't deliberately let people fall all over themselves out of a sorted sense of "they deserve it!"

If anything, the Apostle Paul encourages us to be kind in the face of every sort of adversity: if we must endure, going through troubles, hardships, and distress; in the face of physical torture and imprisonment; during riots; in hard work, physical ailments, tiredness, when people speak bad about us, and when we are sorrowful or lacking financially. We are called to be kind when it's bad, when it's good, and everything in between. Nowhere does the Apostle encourage us to take on a spirit of vengeance, torture, disdain, or to make life harder for other people.

The reason why we are called to be kind is just as important as how we are called to be kind: so Christian ministry will not be discredited. The ministry of God is built upon kindness: the kindness we have received from God and the kindness we are called to show others. God has given us so much in Christ, we too are called to be kind, which proves ministry real and valid. No matter what we are going through, we are always called to be kind, doing for others and making the love of God real to them. We are called to speak in purity, understanding, patience and kindness, because the Holy Spirit is working these things through us, and on our behalf, in a sincere sense of love.

We cannot be kind to anyone without sincere love. Sincere love is love that changes, challenges, and empowers lives. Others can tell when your care is sincere as much as when it's insincere. Kindness is sincere. It does what it does for love's sake, to see lives better and to manifest the ministry of Jesus Christ everywhere we go. Kindness is portable; it travels between circumstances and challenges, and can adapt to every situation where it's required.

2 Corinthians 6:11-13:

We have spoken freely to you, Corinthians, and opened wide our hearts to you. We are not withholding our affection from you, but you are withholding yours from us. As a fair exchange – I speak as to my children – open wide your hearts also.

We can't escape the reality that the world we live in is rather selfish. People consider themselves first, want to do for themselves, and want to receive things without having to give to others. Kindness is a reality call that things aren't all about us. It's not all about what we can get, what we can gain, but about how we can touch lives in more ways, every day.

Some assume that kindness must be some big, grand gesture. The Corinthian church was simply asked to listen and return the affection and kindness extended to them. The Apostle Paul didn't ask for large sums of money, to have a private jet, or for the Corinthians to sacrifice their children on the church altar. He simply asked that they would, in return, open their hearts and extend kindness back. Send a letter of encouragement, make an offering every now and then, have respect for the office of ministry that Paul walked in, be kind to one another, build up the church, and do for one another were all ways they could instill kindness into one another's lives…and those are all things we can, ourselves, do as well to show other people the kindness of God and the love we have as God has endowed us with His kindness.

Kindness and hospitality

Did you know the Bible tells us to be hospitable? Better still, did you know that kindness plays an essential role in hospitality? Maybe that's why we don't see enough of it prevalent today. (Let that sink in!)

3 John 1:7-8:

It was for the sake of the Name that they went out, receiving no help from the pagans. We ought therefore to show hospitality to such people so that we may work together for the truth.

1 Peter 4:9:

Offer hospitality to one another without grumbling.

Romans 12:13:

Share with the Lord's people who are in need. Practice hospitality.

> **HAPPY HARVEST:** Does your church have a hospitality committee? Hospitality committees serve their churches by offering a "fellowship" time after a special service: either coffee and cookies or small snacks, maybe a fellowship lunch, or a banquet for a birthday service. If there is one, join and participate with it. If you don't have one, why don't you take the lead and suggest starting one?

In the first verse above, the Apostle John is praising those who have done work in ministry, especially working among non-believers. He emphasizes the importance of taking care of those in the church, because they could not rely on the pagans to help. The Apostle Peter goes on to state we should offer hospitality without complaint, i.e., with kindness. This tells us that even back then, there were people who did things without kindness, complaining and upset by the suggestion of helping others. The Apostle Paul wasn't advising the church to throw money at people who were needy, but to literally take those who were in serious need into their homes and make sure they had what they needed. In modern times, the advice would be to do the same, or for the church to assist in as much as it is able in helping to provide shelter for spiritual siblings in need. In its very essence, hospitality is the gift of comfort. It exists so those who come into our lives are able to see that God cares about their each and every need, even those that are the most serious in the natural realm.

It's important to start out by saying that even though the Bible does speak of hospitality as a "spiritual gift," not having the gift of hospitality doesn't excuse inhospitable behavior. It's a spiritual gift in the sense that God gives some people the ability to be hospitable in a much easier fashion than others. This doesn't, however, stop the rest of us from being hospitable when it's not as easy for us.

Let me say upfront: I am not the most domestic person in the world, even that I've ever met. From the first printing of this text to today, I am more into cooking than I used to be, and I am more efficient in the kitchen. I've always been a thorough cleaner, but I still wouldn't say that having company over is the easiest thing in the world for me to maintain. It doesn't take long for me to get stressed and overwhelmed while doing that sort of thing. That might not be my spiritual "gift," but when someone came to my door and was homeless, I still did what I could to help them out. I'm great at making sure we create a church atmosphere that is warm and welcoming, and I am far more comfortable doing that. That having been said, if someone is in my home, I will still do my very best to make sure they are comfortable. Even though it might not flow naturally doesn't mean I am exempt from showing kindness to people in that way.

In ancient cultures, people were judged by their ability to be hospitable. Entire nations were judged on their hospitality, and nations with less than stellar hospitality were considered inferior. It was considered the ultimate insult to disregard visitors and to treat others with disregard, especially around hospitality. Making sure people were comfortable, well-cared for during travelling or periods when they are not at home, and well-fed were all vital and essential to life and reputation.

In the early church, the early apostles relied heavily on the kindness of those in the church to take them in and see to it that their needs were met while they were in that area. Nobody came up with the excuse that they couldn't afford it or were unable to do it. They did what needed to be done and assisted their leaders in the work by providing them with the very foundations of kindness in their lives.

How does kindness relate to hospitality? Hospitality is founded on sharing, and sharing is an aspect of kindness. Selfish people aren't kind because they won't share with others. Hospitality is a form of kindness, of love in action, where something is done for the better of someone else. If you don't walk in kindness, you cannot walk in hospitality…and even though it is two thousand years later, God still expects us to open our doors (be it the door of a church or the door of a hotel room) and our hearts to others in kind fellowship.

Kindness killers

We can't talk about kindness without talking about the things that kill kindness. There are some things that hamper its flow and make it so we can't walk in it in our lives like we should. We will probably be quick to see these behaviors in others…but in all things, examine yourself first!

- **Condescending attitudes**: Being condescending is a form of judgment. It is placing oneself high and looking down on others as inferior. However you consider condescending attitudes, they are a major kindness killer. People don't respond to condescending behavior and, let's face it, they do know when someone is speaking down to them.

- **Passive-aggressive behavior**: Passive aggressive behavior consists of indirect actions done to retaliate or 'get back' at others, rather than discussing negative feelings and speaking up about bothersome issues. Passive-aggressive people expect those around them to be "mind readers," anticipating their wants and desires. They get angry and hostile when those wants and desires are not met, even though they never state what they are. Passive-aggressive people may also take their anger about something out on people who have nothing to do with the root situation, whatsoever. There's a lot we could say about passive-aggressive behavior, but it's clear that it isn't kind. It makes being kind to a passive aggressive person very difficult, because you never know how the other person will react.

- **Laziness**: It's impossible to be kind if you aren't willing to be creative and consider the needs, wants, and interests of other people. If you expect everyone to come to you, do the hard part for you, and make being kind easy…it's not going to work.

- **Bitterness**: Being bitter will kill kindness (as well as receiving kindness) because it'll be really clear that nothing's going to break through that veil of anger and hostility.

Producing more excellent fruit

Where are you when it comes to kindness? Where can you do better? Here are some suggestions on ways to produce a more excellent fruit of kindness:

- **Do some research to get some ideas for kindness and different ways to be kind**: Kindness movements exist, especially among others who want to inspire ideas for more and greater kindness in the world today. Check the internet for some current ideas and try some of them out for yourself!

- **Make a point to be more inclusive rather than exclusive**: The basic way most churches operate is through exclusion: if someone want to come to that group, it's fine, as long as those who come into the church look like and act like those who are already there. This is a spirit of exclusivity, whereby people don't feel welcome and do not feel like they can come to church, because they won't "fit in." Jesus was in the temple a total of two times in His recorded three-year ministry: once to read the Scriptures (Luke 4:17) and once to drive out the moneychangers (Matthew 21:12). The rest of the time, Jesus was out, preaching to people, interacting with them, and reaching them with the good news. I think belonging to church is a great thing, and it deeply saddens me that so many people are drifting away from church. At the same time, I understand why so many feel unwelcome, unwanted, and unloved at church. In kindness, we break down this exclusive mindset and make sure the doors of church are welcome to anyone who is interested in attending.

- **Do some "random acts of kindness"**: Random acts of kindness are a great way to reach out to others and to do things without expecting someone to return the favor all the time. Buy a stranger's coffee in the gas station, buy a homeless person a meal and take it to them, put together some "blessing bags" to hand out to the homeless, be creative! Do something nice for others that makes it clear kindness is not dead.

- **Do some "specific acts of kindness"**: I think random acts of kindness are a nice idea, but I think specific acts of kindness are often more important. The people that are often closest to us receive the worst of us or the least of us, and that means we should go out of our way to be kind to them. Instead of having the attitude that "I pay for this" or "I'm already doing this," make a point to do something nice and unexpected for some people who are close to you to show them that you appreciate them.

- **Do tasks without grumbling and complaining**: If there is one thing I dislike as a leader, it is when something needs doing and people complain the whole way through it. That makes it obvious to me that, whether assigned or voluntary, they really don't want to do whatever they are doing. If you want to foster kindness in your life, do the things you do with a good attitude. It makes the people you do them for feel inspired and makes the task itself easier to do.

- **Practice hospitality**: Look for excuses and ways in which to help other people feel more comfortable and "at home." Talk to the new person at church and invite them out for coffee, have some people over to your house for dinner, take someone out for lunch, bring a sick person in the church some soup and some company…and so on. There are lots of opportunities to practice hospitality in this world. You will bless someone else and bless yourself for your actions!

- **Send cards, thank you notes, and letters**: Call me old school, but no technological method replaces sending people greeting cards, handwritten thank you notes, and letters. In kindness, be aware of the things others do for you that are also kind, and be sure to thank them in a way that also reflects true kindness.

Chapter Seven

Goodness

Turn to me and have mercy on me;
grant Your strength in behalf of Your servant
save me, because I serve You, just as my mother did.
Give me a sign of Your goodness,
that my enemies may see it and be put to shame,
for You, O Lord, have helped me and
comforted me.
— Psalm 86:16-17

Assignments:
- Read 2 Thessalonians 1:3-12.
- Clean out your closet and donate gently used clothing that you no longer wear to a charitable organization.
- Call an older family member, ministry colleague, or friend, just to say hi to them.

*I*f we were asked as children, "Do you want to be labeled as good?", the answer would be a resounding no. Being "good" was associated with kids who did things to get noticed and to win the approval of adults. They were the tattletales, brownnosers, and "goody two shoes" of our childhood. They made the concept of goodness, or being good, seem as if it was done to get noticed, for attention, or to be praised.

It didn't help that these were usually the kids who, when no one was looking, behaved worse than the rest of us. They made it a point not to get caught. That way, when we would try to tell the adults in our lives that they were the culprits, no one would believe us.

We developed a negative outlook of "goodness" even though our parents tried to reward us for it. Things like good grades, good behavior, and overall "good performance" rated something extra special in their book. If we did something that was not "good," we were punished for it. From this, we learned to be praised for good behavior, even if there wasn't much behind it. Much like our peer experiences, "goodness" seemed performative, something that was nothing more than surface deep.

The combination of our peers and parental influences both took their toll on our perceptions of goodness. Our conflicts between good and bad soared long into adulthood. We talk now about those who like "bad boys," men who seem rough around the edges and use their partners, but don't seem to like the "good" man who is ready to love and care for them throughout life. We still use the term "bad" to mean someone we really like, and many people are afraid to do good things because they fear the taunts and mockery of others.

No matter what our ideas may be about goodness and how we should manifest it in our own lives, it's obvious the fruit of the Spirit calls us to embody a principle of "goodness." This means we need to sit down and re-think a lot of the things we've attached to goodness that are not really goodness at all and pursue the concept of goodness that God desires us to have. Tattling, brownnosing, being a "goody two shoes" and the like don't reflect Biblical concepts of goodness (in fact, these kinds of behaviors are the exact opposite of what God asks of us when it comes to goodness).

Embodying goodness in the Biblical sense is different from being the opposite of bad. Rather than being about extremes, the Bible always encourages us to be people who maintain a certain balance in our behaviors and personal conducts. Goodness is no different. God asks us, once again, to exemplify certain aspects of what He has done for us (and, is in essence, still doing for us) in our lives as a witness for others. We can't deny that God is good, and that His goodness has done incredible things for us. This means it is time for us to put aside our associations from the social circles of the past, put aside our immature concepts of what it means to be good and of "goodness" in an extended sense, and sincerely step back and learn what God is asking us to do when He speaks clearly on the principle of goodness.

What is goodness?

The term "goodness" is not found frequently in the Bible. In total, it's only found about 19 times. The word "good" is used many more times than "goodness" (610 times), used to identify many different things as being beneficial, pleasant, and likeable. The term "goodness," however, as is found in the fruit of the Spirit, means much, much more than just being likeable, pleasant, or enjoyable. It speaks of being upright in our hearts and lives and being people who reflect that in what we do.

Ephesians 5:1-21:

Follow God's example, therefore, as dearly loved children and walk in the way of love, just as Christ loved us and gave Himself up for us as a fragrant offering and sacrifice to God.

But among you there must not be even a hint of sexual immorality, or of any kind of impurity, or of greed, because these are improper for God's holy people. Nor should there be obscenity, foolish talk or coarse joking, which are out of place, but rather thanksgiving. For of this you can be sure: No immoral, impure or greedy person – such a person is an idolater – has any inheritance in the Kingdom of Christ and of God. Let no one deceive you with empty words, for because of such things God's wrath comes on those who are disobedient. Therefore do not be partners with them.

For you were once darkness, but now you are light in the Lord. Live as children of light (for the fruit of the light consists in all goodness, righteousness and truth) and find out what pleases the Lord. Have nothing to do with the fruitless deeds of darkness, but rather expose them. It is shameful even to mention what the disobedient do in secret. But everything exposed by the light becomes visible – and everything that is illuminated becomes a light. This is why it is said:

> *"Wake up, O sleeper,*
> *rise from the dead,*
> *and Christ will shine on you."*

Be very careful, then, how you live – not as unwise but as wise, making the

> **FOUNDATIONAL FERTILIZER:** A few years ago, I was at an anniversary service a guest praise and worship team took the platform to sing, consisting of three women and one man. I took note that all the women had small, lace coverings on their head (even though that was not required by the church we were at)...and all of the women had on clothes that were inappropriately tight, not fitting properly. Because they had their "heads covered," they thought they were all right in attire. Seeing this made me realize the absurdity in holding on to exterior traditions without truly embracing the inner precepts of goodness that God requires.

most of every opportunity, because the days are evil. Therefore do not be foolish, but understand what the Lord's will is. Do not get drunk on wine, which leads to debauchery. Instead, be filled with the Spirit, speaking to one another with psalms, hymns and songs from the Spirit. Sing and make music in your heart to the Lord, always giving thanks to God the Father for everything, in the Name of our Lord Jesus Christ.

Submit to one another out of reverence for Christ.

- **Goodness imitates God (just as children imitate their parents)**: The Bible tells us God is good. The only One that is truly good is God (Mark 10:18, Luke 18:19). We are called to goodness, to imitate the good nature of God in what we do. Just as little children emulate the behaviors they see in their parents, guardians, and other adults in their lives, so too we should emulate the goodness of God, from our heavenly Father, in everything that we do.

- **Goodness recognizes what is "improper" for God's people**: Debates abound over just what is considered "right" and "wrong" for God's people. Various holiness codes, entertainment regulations, dress codes, and other lists can be found in varying denominations, in parts here and there among different people, almost to the detriment of the church (no one can figure out how we are supposed to interact with one another). Goodness proves that exterior "codes" and long lists of rules don't make people holy; God makes people holy. Long skirts can come up, long pants can come down, and all the many other rules people hold dear as signs of "holiness" can all fail…but goodness will withstand in any situation.

- **Goodness does not engage in offensive or hurtful speech or conduct**: There is nothing wrong with having a good sense of humor. We should have a good sense of humor! Giving the impression that church should be like a graveside funeral has deeply hurt the way Christians are perceived by non-believers. That having been said, we should not be people who are offensive in our speech, making fun of groups of people, or behaving in ways that are disgraceful. All these things are contrary to goodness, which holds itself up in all situations.

> **BUD BREAKS: Goodness**
> #19 *agathosune* [ag-ath-o-soo'-nay]: uprightness of heart and life, goodness, kindness.

- **Goodness doesn't have to hide**: The contrast between darkness and light is the contrast of things hidden (or things needing to be covered up) versus things revealed (or uncovered). If something is in darkness, it needs to be hidden from plain sight due to what it is. Goodness is in the light, living in the light, because it does not need to hide what it does from anyone.

- **Goodness, righteousness, and truth work together**: Goodness works with righteousness (the manifestation of righteous deeds) and truth because being in goodness means that the deeds one does will manifest God's righteousness and His truth.

- **Goodness is obedient (and has no partnership with the disobedient)**: Obedience is a loaded word, one many like to avoid. Being obedient is an essential part of Christianity, in many ways and contexts. Above all things, in every situation we are in, we should gain a greater sense of obedience to God, doing what He asks of us. This is where things get tricky: that means we should not be dealing in partnerships where people are deliberately disobedient to God, or disobedient in general. Disobedient people lead to hostility with others and make it impossible for goodness to flourish in such an environment.

- **Goodness is fruitful**: Goodness is productive, spreading to others, and keeping a healthy vine to expand and grow, affecting and loving others in the way we live.

- **Goodness is all about conduct**: There's a long list of advice in Ephesians 5 about conduct, advising us to be careful in how we live. We see goodness prevalent in how we live our lives. More than being about what we do (which was what kindness was), goodness is who we are, how we live, and how we choose to represent the Kingdom of God in every choice we make.

- **Goodness submits one to another**: We talk a lot about submission in limited contexts, but the Bible is clear that we should be submitting, each one of us, to everyone in the Body of Christ. This is about being accountable and treating one another with principles of goodness, including dignity and respect.

If kindness as spoken of in the last chapter is what we do, goodness is who we are…or at least, who we should be aspiring to be.

The walls to our spiritual house

As we continue in the development of our spiritual house, goodness is the drywall and walls of the home. Even though the walls must rest on a frame, a foundation, and other essential aspects of the home, the walls also keep the home standing strong and protect those in the home from the physical damage of the elements. The walls do not work on their own, but work with other aspects of the building in order to keep the house in check. A house can't stand without walls!

The same is true with goodness. It doesn't work by itself alone. Goodness requires all the other fruit of the Spirit to stand with it and enhance the life of the believer: as a protection, a shield, and a defense.

Goodness shall follow me...

Psalm 23 is used all sorts of different ways, often to instill a sense of God's providence and comfort. The one thing that we don't often realize about Psalm 23 is that it reveals a lot about goodness to us, especially the goodness of God. If in goodness we are supposed to be imitating God's goodness, Psalm 23 should tell us about the ways goodness should reflect in our lives.

Psalm 23:1:

The LORD is my shepherd, I lack nothing.

We like the image of a shepherd for a wall hanging, but do we understand why the image of "shepherd" was used so intimately in connection with God? It's because shepherding was a difficult job! The shepherd's life revolved around caring for sheep. Sheep are not the smartest of animals. They don't have good sense and will easily wander off and get themselves into trouble without the right guidance. This means guidance of sheep is almost constant, especially in the early stages, having to protect and oversee the sheep. Not only are sheep relatively stupid, they are also extremely stubborn. They are willful and want their own way, and want to do things, even if they are bad for them. Sheep need their shepherd to constantly watch and care for them, keep bugs and insects out of their fur and their faces, protect them from unseen forces, and work with them for their entire lives. Sheep don't want because they have their shepherd.

> **PRUNING POINTS:** Almost 20 years ago, I preached a message titled, "The Lord Is My Shepherd...But Still Do I Want." In it, I explored modern discontent that desires to amass more and more things in the Name of God, but never seems satisfied. Do you find yourself always wanting something else? If so, maybe it's time to look at why.

Saying God is our shepherd is as much about Him as it is about us. It tells us that as difficult as we are, God's goodness is bigger and better than we are on our worst day. As our Shepherd, we need His persistently good presence in our lives. It's not just about what He gives to us or what He does for us, but the fact that He, in His very nature, is the very definition of goodness. No matter how bad we are, His goodness is greater.

Goodness sticks with things. It doesn't give up because it's too difficult or too hard. This can apply to dealing with people who are a little much to handle, or it can apply to any task God assigns to us that seems to be difficult or hard.

Psalm 23:2-3:

He makes me lie down in green pastures,
He leads me beside quiet waters,
   He refreshes my soul.
He guides along the right paths
   for His Name's sake.

In God's goodness, He provides for us. God's provision is not simply squeaking by, but of being more than adequate. The goodness of God is above and beyond, bringing a complete sense of peace and purpose. God's restoration heals both body and soul and guides the follower of God unto the paths of righteousness.

We learn God is good for His Name's sake: in other words, what God does is associated with Him, and He goes above and beyond to make sure that what He does is associated with the best of the best. There is no lack in God, and His provision is sure.

In goodness, what we do is also associated with what God does. There are endless stories of people who gave up on God because they were mistreated by Christians and, by extension, the church. This is part of why it is so important that we live according to goodness, and that we function by goodness and do things that are good for others. They are watching us, taking notes, and judging God by how they assess us. What we do is not just for us, but for God, and goodness remembers that.

Psalm 23:4:

Even though I walk
   through the darkest valley,
I will fear no evil,
   for You are with me;

Your rod and Your staff,
  they comfort me.

Goodness is a constant reminder of God's presence in our lives, no matter what we are going through. Because God is the One Who is good, goodness is one of the ways God's manifesting presence makes Him known to us. This passage does prove that things will happen in this life that are not enjoyable, but that does not mean God is not good or that bad things can never happen. On the contrary, even though dark and difficult things happen, God is still good, and we have nothing to fear. In goodness, we find comfort. In living by goodness, we not only find reassurance, we also are able to give comfort to others. It's impossible to offer something to people that you haven't received yourself, and in this very same way, we can't reassure people that we have nothing to fear because God is with us if we don't realize this ourselves.

Psalm 23:5-6:

You prepare a table before me
  in the presence of my enemies.
You anoint my head with oil;
  my cup overflows.
Surely goodness and love will follow me
  all the days of my life,
and I will dwell in the house of the LORD forever.

In God's goodness, He restores us above our enemies and honors us in front of them. He sets us apart for a purpose, making sure we are ready and able to do His work. Because He does all these things, we can trust that His goodness and love will follow us, all throughout our lives. Being able to dwell in His house is enough, because we know His blessing rests on those of us who are in there.

In echoing his goodness, we rejoice when someone finds victory in their lives. "Enemies" take many forms; they are not just people, but the vices, voices, and habits we have that follow us long after we are saved. Goodness rejoices in every victory; in the callings we all have as believers and hopes to see us in our purpose; and makes sure that goodness and mercy follow, as we are all able to dwell in God's house for eternity.

Attributes of goodness

Since goodness is who we are, it has certain characteristics by which it can be identified. We've all met people we knew were not good, but also met many people who were supposedly the "salt of the earth" good who were not, in reality, very good people. Goodness has a look; it goes with the essence of life that one has when they are walking in the Spirit and developing this fruit in their lives.

2 Thessalonians 1:3-4:

We ought always to thank God for you, brothers and sisters, and rightly so, because your faith is growing more and more, and the love all of you have for one another is increasing. Therefore, among God's churches we boast about your perseverance and faith in all the persecutions and trials you are enduring.

Goodness is something that serves to encourage the body of believers, one to another. We can all testify to how hard life can be at times. It's so nice to receive the encouragement and support of others who are also going through, each in their own way. By goodness, our faith increases, and our love increases. Such pushes us on to greater perseverance, in any trial we may go through.

Goodness is how we get through trials. We don't get through them by pulling the wool over our eyes, but being persistent in our goodness, not allowing outside things to change who we are, as we go through whatever we are going through. We don't wish them away or positively think our problems into nonexistence; rather, we get through by goodness. Thanks to the goodness of others, we band together and go through everything we must get through.

2 Thessalonians 1:5-10:

All this is evidence that God's judgment is right, and as a result you will be counted worthy of the Kingdom of God, for which you are suffering. God is just: He will pay back trouble to those who trouble you and give relief to you who are troubled, and to us as well. This will happen when the Lord Jesus is revealed from heaven in blazing fire with His powerful angels. He will punish those who do not know God and do not obey the Gospel of our Lord Jesus. They will be punished with everlasting destruction and shut out from the presence of the Lord and from the majesty of His power on the day He comes to be glorified in His holy people and to be marveled at among all those who have believed. This includes you, because you believed our testimony to you.

Goodness is frequently contrasted with things that are wrong, because God wants to know that goodness is not for naught. Goodness does count for something, even if we can't see it right now. If nobody knows what we do, God does. In the long run, He is keeping our "score," so to speak. Everything done to offend, cause harm, and work against goodness will come home to roost. Those who do wrong will reap what they sow, and those who do good will also reap a harvest for their well-doing.

The goodness of God persists through the difficulties and through these times when testimony is being written. That's how we come out on the other side, reporting what we have learned in our trials and what we did wrong and right.

2 Thessalonians 1:11-12:

With this in mind, we constantly pray for you, that our God may make you worthy of His calling, and that by His power He may bring to fruition your evert desire for goodness and your every deed prompted by faith. We pray this so that the Name of our Lord Jesus may be glorified in you, and you in Him, according to the grace of our God and the Lord Jesus Christ.

The fruits of goodness are constant prayer, walking worthy of His calling, and God fulfilling every good purpose within each one of us. The conduit by which God works His goodness is faith, because in goodness, we are directed more and more by it. The glorification of Jesus Christ comes as we walk in goodness and follow His grace all through our lives, unto eternity.

Goodness and suffering

We've all heard people say, "If God is good, why is there suffering?" or "If God is good, why are Christians not good?"

Some people ask these questions with genuine intent. I believe there is a question of contradiction in the minds of people who do not really understand how God can be good, but things can go wrong, things can be bad at times and sometimes we have events occur (such as natural disasters) for which no one seems to have an answer.

> **POWER POLLINATION:** Instead of hoping God gets someone out of a hard situation by some outlandish means, what can you do to help them? You could very well be the way God reaches out to someone else!

The answer to the question itself is weighty, and could fill a book, all by itself. For the sake of our conversation here, confusion exists because associate "good" with things being easy or always going a certain way. As we associate goodness with God, we associate our concept of good with God. In our minds, this means we shouldn't have to suffer, and God should in His might and power, always utilize His goodness to ease human discomforts.

The problem with this logic is that God never promised to use His might and power to give us an easy life. From the very beginning, human beings have always wanted their own way, without any complications. Sin exists in this world because of this early transgression. The existence of sin isn't because God isn't good, but because we, as human beings, often don't know and refuse to learn our own limitations. If we are honest with ourselves, God wouldn't be good if He didn't let us taste the consequences of our own actions and come into a deeper experience with the realities of how far-reaching sin can be through the results of such throughout both human action and the cosmos itself.

It is true that God is "good" to us in the sense that we receive blessings from Him. Scripture teaches us that all that is good comes from God. We should never forget, however, that the "goodness" we speak of is more than just things all nicely going our way. God's goodness takes the form of uprightness of moral character, all the way unto perfection. This means that, in His perfection, God operates by means we do not always understand.

One of the ways that seems complicated to us, but is part of His goodness, is that He has given human beings free will. In God's governance, people have the choice to follow Him or follow their own ways. People don't always follow the will of God. In their sinfulness, they choose to disobey God. This can have effects on others, including suffering. We all have the choice to properly use and care for the things He has given to each one of us (material resources, natural resources, spiritual resources) or to disregard them and follow our own path. People sin because they refuse to follow God. Good people are caught in suffering because they live with other people and none of us is an island. The consequences of sin are often far-reaching and stretch far beyond the bounds that are comfortable and desirable for each of us. There is suffering because there is sin.

God, however, is right where He always is. Instead of assuming God does not exist because bad things happen (or perceiving God to be cruel), we should seek Him for revelation, seeking a deeper wisdom and understanding in each situation. Psalm 142:7 says:

Set me free from my prison,
  that I may praise Your Name.
Then the righteous will gather about me
  because of Your goodness to me.

Instead of thinking that God isn't doing enough (or enough of the right thing by us), we should set ourselves free from the prison found in this attitude and ask God to reveal Himself to us in His full goodness. The more we recognize God is good, the more we will cleave unto Him and begin to develop needed attributes to change into a deeper sense of His Image.

How we do our "righteous acts"

There are many things the Bible discusses that we could classify as "character flaws." If we are to develop the fruit of goodness, these must be changed. One such example is the need to do things in front of everyone to get praise and accolades for the "good" we do.

Let's be real for a few minutes, honest with ourselves. All of us, every single one from the greatest to the least, enjoys receiving praise from others. It's nice to feel seen and appreciated by others, especially if we are doing something for them. Preachers and ministers love getting up in the pulpit, helps ministers love it when the preacher thanks them in front of the entire congregation for their commendable service, and lay members love being acknowledged for chairing a committee or several years of notable church attendance. All of us enjoy compliments on our appearance, clothes, hair, shoes, nails, or something we have that sets us apart from others. It's not wrong to acknowledge the things others do well. In connection with that, there is nothing wrong with enjoying a compliment. The way we accept compliments says a lot about us. People who are so self-depreciating that they can't even accept someone's kind words about them haven't found their needed balance to be effective witnesses for the Lord.

The issue with compliments comes in when we seek that admiration more than we seek the approval of God. If our only purpose in doing notable or good things is to be noticed by other people, we are doing things with the wrong motives.

Matthew 6:1-4:

"Be careful not to practice your righteousness in front of others to be seen by them. If you do, you will have no reward from your Father in heaven.

"So when you give to the needy, do not announce it with trumpets, as the hypocrites do in the synagogues and on the streets, to be honored by others. Truly I tell you, they have received their reward in full. But when you give to the needy, do not let your left hand know what your right hand is doing, so that your giving may be in secret. Then your Father, Who sees what

> **HAPPY HARVEST:** I believe every church and ministry should exercise the commands of Matthew 25 throughout the year. Is there some way you can facilitate a food drive? Offer a meal for a needy family? Provide school supplies where they are most needed? If your church doesn't have these events, maybe nobody has suggested them. If needed, suggest teaming up with another ministry for these different projects. We can do more if we work together!

is done in secret, will reward you."

There's a fine line between doing something that seems good and doing something that is, in fact, really good. The difference lies in motives. Goodness doesn't do things with the wrong motives. In fact, goodness does things just for the sake of doing them: because they are the right thing to do, the needed thing to do, in that very moment, at that time. God wants us to embrace goodness because things need doing, not dependent on the human rewards or accolades that might come along with it. Throughout history, the church has flourished thanks to people who did things, even though we have no record of their names. Thanks to them, the faith has continued down through to today. It benefits us to make sure that when we are do things, we do them for goodness sake, not personal sake.

Goodness, dignity, and respect

Perhaps the greatest ways that goodness manifests are in the forms of dignity and respect. Even though much of the church world does not appear interested in human rights, dignity and respect are an essential part of the Gospel message. If we truly believe that each human being is created in the image of God (Genesis 1:26-27), then we believe people are worthy of being treated with dignity and respect. These attributes are not dependent on what the people in question have done or are doing, just like their creation in God's image is not dependent upon those things. Jesus Himself was interested in the social issues that affected people as much as He was in those areas that affected their souls. We can see that we are to do the same within our focus on goodness, as is found in Matthew 25:34-40:

"Then the King will say to those on His right, 'Come, you who are blessed by My Father; take your inheritance, the Kingdom prepared for you since the creation of the world. For I was hungry and you gave Me something to eat, I was thirsty and you gave Me something to drink, I was a stranger and you invited Me in, I needed clothes and you clothed Me, I was sick and you looked after Me, I was in prison and you came to visit Me.'

"Then the righteous will answer Him, 'Lord, when did we see You hungry and feed You, or thirsty and give You something to drink? When did we see You a stranger and invite You in, or needing clothes and clothe You? When did we see You sick or in prison and go to visit You?'

"The King will reply, 'Truly I tell you, whatever you did for one of the least of these brothers and sisters of Mine, you did for Me.'"

Those who are truly good do things for goodness' sake. Those who received the inheritance mentioned did things because they were the right thing to do at the right time, and for no other reason. They cared about people who were without, who lived in dire conditions, lived in poverty, who didn't have what someone else had. Goodness regards the lives of people as important, no matter who they are or where they come from.

Beyond the initial literal headings we find in Matthew 25 are a number of subheadings that also relate to care, interest, and the needs of others. There are too many to list here. The bottom line of the passage is that whenever we sincerely see the dignity and respect in anyone – including those society might deem as the "least of these" – we participate in a powerful form of goodness that transforms this world. It might not fix all the world's problems, but right there, in that moment, it addresses a need that must be met in a practical way.

The world needs – demands – yearns for – the church to lead the way in dignity and respect. Even though we may not agree with the things everyone does, we can be good to others. We can listen when they speak, empathize with the struggles they have, work to make people's lives better, and we can meet the needs that exist, in any variety of ways as God instructs. Stepping up and function through the work of Matthew 25 opens doors for vital and extensive outreach, with many ways to show the world that God is good.

Producing more excellent fruit

Where are you when it comes to goodness? Where can you do better? Here are some suggestions on ways to produce a more excellent fruit of goodness:

- **Take part in some social Gospel activities**: Social Gospel activities are those that relate to the action of Gospel work that help improve the social condition of individuals. Visiting sick people in the hospital, working with inmates, participating in homeless outreach, food banks, community feeding programs, building houses for homeless families, advocating for safe working conditions, access to clean water, representing the marginalized in protection and community education, creating community, being agents of inclusion, and so on and so forth are all ways the Gospel is "preached" through social activities. Take part in one – or some – of these different activities to see the important ways that goodness can be mobilized.

- **Let go of needless and endless debates and disagreements**: This relates to peace, patience, love, joy, and kindness, but it also relates to goodness. It shows you are not afraid to be the one to go first when it comes to walking away from things that need to be let go. If we are really in the Gospel for Jesus' sake and not to be right, or have other people think we are wonderful or agree with us, we will be willing to let go of the many trivial and needless things that people often debate and argue about, because they have no purpose.

- **Be true evangelizers of the faith**: Evangelism is about both belief and action. This means: it is about what we do for others as much as what we tell others about the Lord. Every one of us needs to know how to give testimony, how to talk about Gospel issues, and how to handle controversial issues with a sense of goodness. The only way we can do this is to show people we love them as much as we claim. If we tell people all day long that God loves them and then we turn them away when they have a need we can reasonably meet, we are the ones turning them away. God asks that in our spirit of true evangelism, we are not just hearers of the Word, but doers, as well (James 1:22).

- **Do a good deed and make a point not to get found out**: One of the greatest ways to practice goodness is to do a good deed and make sure you don't get credit for doing it. Whatever you pick to do, remember, you must remain completely anonymous...nobody can ever know you are behind it!

- **Look at politics objectively**: I meet too many people with many political opinions. They are quick to defend or debate their political beliefs based on those of their own party. In the process, they turn people off, because people think their political opinions mirror the way God feels about some of these issues. God does tell us we are to respect those in governmental authority (Romans 13:1), but nowhere does He tell us to put our confidences in them. It is not the government's job to do the Kingdom's job! Believing a political party is going to solve the problems of a world or a nation is dangerous territory. Rather than advocating politics, advocate Kingdom participation and character.

- **Make sure your tithes and offerings are paid promptly**: Ministries have a hard time doing outreach programs when their leaders must also work secular jobs to pay ministry expenses on top of their own personal life costs. The participation of every member in a church to pay tithes and offerings – each month, up front, in full, without complaint or argument – is essential for churches to flourish in outreach ministries and in social Gospel work for the community. Walking in goodness starts in practical ways that all of us can do, especially if we haven't been doing them for awhile.

- **Invite someone to come to church with you**: If you are afraid or ashamed to take someone to church with you, there is something wrong with the church you attend. You should always feel ready to bring people to church! Church attendance is a great way to share with them and allow them the chance to also share in the love and fellowship present there. Those who need to know God, need to rekindle their relationship with Him, and those who need to feel His presence should all be aware of a sense of goodness every time they walk into a ministry fellowship with you.

Chapter Eight

Faithfulness

"For I, the LORD, love justice;
I hate robbery and wrongdoing.
In My faithfulness I will reward My people
and make an everlasting covenant with them.
Their descendants will be known among the nations
and their offspring among the peoples.
All who see them will acknowledge
that they are a people the LORD has blessed."
- Isaiah 61:8-9

Assignments:
- Read 3 John 1:1-8.
- Pray for someone going through a difficult time.
- Make it through a current trial without complaining.

We love the principle of faithfulness, until it comes down to us.
Silent pause for reflection

I know that last statement will step on a few toes, but the reason it hurts is because it's true. We like the idea of faithful spouses, friends, employees, children, and church members, until we start talking about ourselves. We look out over the world and condemn the way people fail to follow through on their commitments. It's shocking when people attend a church a few times and then stop. We're appalled to hear about people who are part of something, but don't give to it. We can't believe the number of people who skip out on Sunday services or take off from work because they don't feel like working that day. There's no end to our commentaries on everything that's wrong with "the world."

Then we are quick to excuse our lapses of faithfulness. When we fail to be faithful, we use every excuse we can conceive: forgetfulness, other people's lapses or bad behavior, working too much, family obligations, or being overly tired as the reasons why we failed to be faithful in some (or many) ways. It probably doesn't help that entertainment means don't encourage faithful behavior. Half-naked celebrities spend money however they want, doing whatever they want, and leaving relationships, jobs, commitments, and other promises in the wake whenever the mood strikes them. Following their lead, the celebrity church scene also knows how to draw a crowd, but struggles in key areas of faithfulness, including in marriage and ministry integrity.

The purpose of this chapter isn't to judge, but to call every one of us to personal examination of faithfulness. In discussing the fruit of the Spirit, we are quick to talk about love, joy, and peace, but often leave the world of faithfulness for another time and place. Regardless, faithfulness matters. It's not just for old dogs (it goes beyond Old Yeller, Lassie, Rin Tin Tin, Snoopy, and Beethoven) and misty-eyed memories of long ago, where people kept their word and stayed together as friends and families no matter how much they all hated each other (like grandma and grandpa used to talk about). Whether marriages, secret kid's clubs, adult friendships, dating, church connections, employers and employees, God and His people, or any relationship in any form, faithfulness is paramount to ensuring a lasting bond and a sense of trust. If we want to be people that others can rely upon and trust, we must be faithful.

As we will see in this chapter, faithfulness is about a lot more than having a good reputation or being social with others. Faithfulness is a condition of our faith! It defines our relationship with God and with others and is the essence of what God asks of us in our character. We can choose to be many things in this life, but it is clear and assured that God asks us to be, above all things, people of faith.

Yet with this important and essential aspect of our faith life, faithfulness is a seldom explored aspect of our spirituality. We try to tackle faith without it, but that means we don't understand it very well. We don't talk about what it means to be faithful and the many ways we can express our faith in our daily lives. Faithfulness proves that being people of faith is not just reserved for church leaders, pastors, apostles, prophets, evangelists, teachers, and the appointment ministries. We are all called to live lives that reflect faith, from the greatest of us to the least. That way, when the roll of faith heroes is called in days to come, we will find our names on it. By so doing, we embrace the complete principle of faith and living by faith in each and every situation. It is possible to live by faith. Faithfulness is the way we can do that, one step and situation at a time.

What is faithfulness?

In studying the Greek word for "faithfulness," I was fascinated to learn it is the Greek word for "faith." Some translations of the Bible do translate this aspect of the fruit of the Spirit as "faith," and they are correct for doing so in keeping with the translation. In studying the concept, however, I understand why the word "faithfulness" is also frequently used, without inaccuracy or contradiction. Faithfulness is the condition of being in faith, of our continued efforts toward the things we hope for, but do not see right now. It focuses on the "who" (God) versus the "what" (a miracle, breakthrough, etc.). (We will discuss this more a little later.)

It wouldn't be right to talk about the definition of faith and not include portions of Hebrews 11. Called the "Heavenly Hall of Heroes," it is much, much more than a random listing of people who were "good enough." It is a list of people who were faithful, who lived by their faith because they trusted and believed in God beyond their theologies, beyond the things that they were "taught" about God and embraced the lives He called them to lead.

Hebrews 11:1-3:

Now faith is confidence in what we hope for and assurance about what we do not see. This is what the ancients were commended for.

By faith we understand that the universe was formed at God's command, so that what is seen was not made out of what was visible.

The whole of Hebrews 11 provides examples of the definition of faith we find in Hebrews 11:1. Faith is defined of being sure of what we hope for and certain of what we do not see. Other translations define it as the substance (stuff) of things that are hoped for, the evidence (proof) of what is not seen. This is a complex ontological statement that basically says faith proves itself. We can talk all day long about having faith, or believing in faith, or trying to define faith, but in the end, faith proves itself. We can go a step further to say faith is proved by faithfulness. It is proven as we live out our faith, as what we claim to know about God is made visible in how we live our lives. The first example the writer gives is through the creation of the universe. Everything we see around us exists because of Gods command. It does not exist independently of itself. Creation proves the things we can't see are real, because what we see was created out of what we cannot see. Thus, creation proves that our faithfulness is not void, because things seen came from things unseen.

Hebrews 11:4-16:

By faith Abel brought God a better offering than Cain did. By faith he was commended as righteous when God spoke well of his offerings. And by faith Abel still speaks, even though he is dead.

By faith Enoch was taken from this life, so that he did not experience death: "He could not be found, because God had taken him away." For before he was taken, he was commended as one who pleased God. And without faith it is impossible to please God, because anyone who comes to Him must believe that He exists and that He rewards those who earnestly seek Him.

By faith Noah, when warned about things not yet seen, in holy fear built an ark to save his family. By his faith he condemned the world and became heir of the righteousness that is in keeping with faith.

By faith Abraham, when called to go to a place he would later receive as his inheritance, obeyed and went, even though he did not know where he was going. By faith he made his home in the Promised Land like a stranger in a foreign country; he lived in tents, as did Isaac and Jacob, who were heirs with him of the same promise. For he was looking forward to the city with foundations, whose architect and builder is God. And by faith even Sarah, who was past childbearing age, was enabled to bear children because she considered Him faithful Who made the promise. And so from this one man, and he as good as dead, came descendants as numerous as the stars in the sky and as countless as the sand on the seashore.

> **BUD BREAKS: Faith** #4102 - *pistis* [pis'-tis]: conviction of the truth of anything, belief; in the NT of a conviction or belief respecting man's relationship to God and divine things, generally with the included idea of trust and holy fervor born of faith and joined with it.

All these people were still living by faith when they died. They did not receive the things promised; they only saw them and welcomed them from a distance, admitting that they were foreigners and strangers on earth. People who say such things show that they are looking for a country of their own. If they had been thinking of the country they had left, they would have had opportunity to return. Instead, they were longing for a better country – a heavenly one. Therefore God is not ashamed to be called their God, for He has prepared a city for them.

Looking at these people and looking at the definition of faith, we can understand the following:

- **Faithfulness operates by faith**: If we don't have faith, we can't live by faith, which means we can't be faithful people. If we truly believe in God and know He is good to His Word, we will reflect that in the decisions and choices we make.

- **Faithfulness doesn't need to see immediate results to operate**: Hebrews 11 points out that all the people listed above died and did not see the promise they were to receive. Abraham did not ever see his generations and generations of offspring alive, because he died. Enoch walked with God, but lived in a time when many did not walk with God. Abel offered a better offering than Cain, but he was killed before he was able to walk in the benefits of that faith. The ultimate promise they all missed was the birth of Jesus Christ, the Redeemer. Even though they did not see that (or things immediate to them), they still believed and trusted God. If we want to be faithful people, we can't always be looking for an immediate or a quick fix.

- **Faithfulness is seen and operates by the things we do and the choices we make**: We debate a lot about being people who "believe," but what does it mean to believe? Does it mean we adopt a certain theological or philosophical point that has no application or practicality? Does it mean we are hostile when we don't agree with what someone else believes or does? Does it mean we say we "believe" but that has no impact on our lives? The answer to these questions, considering faithfulness, is no. What we believe is seen as we are faithful to Him.

- **Faithfulness pleases God**: Even though Abel, Noah, Enoch, Abraham, Sarah, and others did not always enjoy what they had to experience, they remained faithful. It was not easy to please God, walk away from families and the familiar, to stand out and do something completely unknown and different from everyone else. The faithful, however, please God, when it's easy and when it's hard.

- **Faithfulness reaps a reward**: God rewards faithfulness, both in this life and in the next. Even though we may not see the fullness of what God promises, we can know God is with us and He is working all things together for our good.

- **Faithfulness believes the impossible**: Just because it doesn't seem possible in the natural doesn't mean it is impossible with God. While God is not an unreasonable God, He is also the God of things we can't imagine and can't conceive of our own doing. If you are in Him, then you also believe that incredible things can happen, even unto those things that people say can never happen.

- **Faithfulness sets you apart**: Abraham, Noah, Enoch, Abel, Sarah and the rest of those in the Bible were people who did things that were different. They didn't readily fit in with the crowd. The things they did were so unusual they stood out. Others could point to them as "odd" or "strange." If you are going to be a faithful person, your faithfulness will set you apart. You may very well seem od or strange to others. The things you do won't make sense, and this might mean you won't fit in everywhere you go.

- **Faithfulness looks and believes for better things**: With faith, we believe right now for things we know will come. Our actions in faithfulness manifest that which we believe for in the future, making them real, right now.

The flooring and windows in our spiritual house

> **POWER POLLINATION:** Team up with an accountability partner and keep track of the ways that you can live by your faith in more obvious ways.

Where would we be in a home without floors and windows? In small, dark boxes on a concrete slab! Floors give stability while windows let in light. Faithfulness gives us stability, providing a surface on which to plant our feet and walk steadily, letting light into our lives. In our spiritual lives and especially in these times, we need the stability and light that only faithfulness can offer.

The just shall live by faith

We've heard it said for years, "the just shall live by faith." It doesn't ever get much deeper than that proclamation, however. We don't talk about what it means to be "the just who live by faith" or what living by faith means or looks like. If we want to understand what faithfulness is, we need to understand the statement, "the just shall live by faith." or this, we go to Romans 1:14-17:

I am obligated both to Greeks and non-Greeks, both to the wise and the foolish. That is why I am so eager to preach the Gospel also to you who are at Rome.

I am not ashamed of the Gospel, because it is the power of God that brings salvation to everyone who believes: first to the Jew, then to the Gentile. For in the Gospel the righteousness of God is revealed – a righteousness that is by faith from first to last, just as it is written: "The righteous will live by faith."

First thing to note: the Bible doesn't say we will believe by faith or create long-winded doctrines by faith. It also doesn't say we will hide behind our faith or use it as an excuse to avoid doing what needs to be done. Surely, there's nothing wrong with believing, doctrine, or doing things because of our faith. These things aren't wrong in themselves, but it doesn't say these are the things we will live by as believers. The Bible tells us if we are righteous, we will

> **PRUNING POINTS:** It's easy to assume your relationship with God is fine, especially if you judge it by material standards. The Bible tells us, however, that it rains on the just and the unjust alike (meaning material standards aren't a reflection of our faith). Are you obedient to God, even when it costs you something?

live by faith, or we could also say, we will live by faithfulness.

Without making the concept more complicated than it needs to be, this means our faith will show in the way we interact with others and handle many things that come along in this life – both difficult and joyful (and everything in between). Faithfulness displays our relationship with God before the world, aiming to be pleasing before Him before all others, and a testimony to the world.

Attributes of faithfulness

If kindness is what we do and goodness is who we are, then faithfulness is our character. It is the fruit of a life lived in Christ, built upon the essential foundations of faith that help us believe for the impossible, trust for our necessities, and live life in a completely different fashion from the general world. 3 John 1:1-4 says:

The elder,

To my dear friend Gaius, whom I love in the truth.

Dear friend, I pray that you may enjoy good health and that all may go well with you, even as your soul is getting along well. It gave me great joy when some believers came and testified about your faithfulness to the truth, telling how you continue to walk in it. I have no greater joy than to hear that my children are walking in the truth.

The Apostle John starts out his letter by commending friends who he loves in truth, because they were people of the truth. Faithfulness is noted by people who are of the truth. We can believe in various theories and theologies all day long, but it is different when we are people of the truth. We recognize the way, the truth, and the life to be Jesus Christ, the Word made flesh Who dwelt among people on this earth (John 1:1,14). This means we can have a relationship with truth, made possible through the work of faithfulness. If we have faith, then we desire to follow the way, the truth, and the life. This will manifest as we are people who will be truthful; who will desire to lead unto the way of truthfulness; and that we will continue to walk in the truth. We are not just committed to the truth in every situation, but the truth in the work of Jesus Christ. Such is cause for joy, because it is a walk of faithfulness and promise.

3 John 1:5-8:

Dear friend, you are faithful in what you are doing for the brothers and sisters, even though they are strangers to you. They have told the church about your love. Please send them on their way in a manner that honors God. It was for the sake of the Name that they went out, receiving no help from the pagans. We ought therefore to show hospitality to such men so that we may work together for the truth.

I'm sure you remember this passage during talk about hospitality in our earlier chapter on kindness. Hospitality was an essential aspect of the work of kindness, and now we will look at the principle of faithfulness present in these verses. John commended believers who were faithful to leaders doing the work of the Gospel, whether they were their own personal leaders. Their faith allowed them to be faithful, because these individuals who were preaching the Gospel were also being faithful. This means their efforts of kindness displayed their faithfulness, not just to the work of ministry, or the leaders at hand, but also to God. They supported whoever needed their support, when they needed that support. Going the extra mile is a mark of faithfulness, because there is no question as to what one believes. Faithfulness follows things through to the very end and beyond, recognizing such commitment because faith is a walk of eternity.

Faithfulness defines our relationship with God

We could simply define faithfulness as the condition of being in faith and in our continued efforts of faith. It, therefore, becomes a measure of just where we are with God. How committed are we to the Gospel? Just as the believers mentioned in 3 John 1:5-8, those were individuals who were ready to make sure that their belief in God was confirmed and sure, no matter what happened or what needs .

This is how faithfulness works. We need to be people who are ready, willing, and able to do whatever God asks of us, at any time. We need to be willing to go the extra mile for those who are in the faith, and we need to be people who keep our commitments, who fulfill our assignments, and who walk in humility. Psalm 40:4-10 says:

Blessed is the one
 who trusts in the LORD,
who does not look to the proud,
 to those who turn aside to false gods.
Many, LORD my God, are the wonders You have done,
 the things You planned for us.
None can compare with You;
 were I to speak and tell of your deeds,
 they would be too many to declare.

Sacrifice and offering you did not desire –
 but my ears You have opened –
 burnt offerings and sin offerings You did not require.
Then I said, "Here I am, I have come –
 it is written about me in the scroll.
I desire to do Your will, my God;
 Your law is within my heart."

I proclaim your saving acts in the great assembly;
 I do not seal my lips, LORD,
 as You know.
I do not hide Your righteousness in my heart;

I speak of Your faithfulness and your saving help.
I do not conceal Your love and Your faithfulness
  from the great assembly.

The faithful recognize God's faithfulness. Our faithfulness to Him does not rest in outward sacrifices. God desires we are consistent in our faith, as faithful unto Him. Such shows in our lives, which doesn't require constant sacrifices to make up for the wrongdoing we do. God doesn't require His people to make a huge show to try and prove their faith. He knows – and teaches us – that our faith is proven through faithful commitments, trusting the whole time that what we have not seen is yet true and that what we hope for is still yet to come.

A belief in God beyond mere doctrine

Faithfulness takes our belief in God to the next level. Most churches have certain statements of faith and doctrinal beliefs that govern the ideas presented among their adherents. People attend these churches because they believe in the on-paper teachings about God and faith, and they desire to ascribe to those beliefs. In and of themselves, there is nothing wrong with having beliefs or trying to describe different doctrinal beliefs on paper. All of us should be able to articulate our beliefs, even acknowledging that what we say in words is no comparison to the grandeur of our God in heaven. Faithfulness, however, goes beyond these different terms, words, ideas, and concepts that we try to ascribe to God. Every description we have of our relationship with God falters at some point in time when God calls us to be faithful in a way that stands contrary to everything we believe on paper. Our relationship with the Father should be beyond that which is doctrinal, following faithfulness wherever it leads, however it leads. This is why Proverbs 3:3-4 says:

Let love and faithfulness never leave you;
  bind them around your neck,
  write them on the tablet of your heart.
Then you will win favor and a good name

in the sight of God and man.

The book of Jonah teaches us about this very concept – and the call to faithfulness. The Prophet Jonah was not faithful without a struggle. We all know the story of Jonah well: God told Jonah what to do, Jonah didn't want to do it, Jonah didn't do it, Jonah wound up in the belly of a whale, Jonah got out of the whale, Jonah went to Nineveh, Nineveh repented, Nineveh was not destroyed, and Jonah got mad at God. Jonah knew what God asked of him, but he didn't fear disobeying what God asked of him. Why? His "doctrine," his concept of God on paper, assured him that he didn't need to worry about such disobedience. Nineveh was full of Assyrians, who were occupiers of the Jews in Jonah's day. Sending a message of repentance – and then recognizing God did indeed honor their repentance – wasn't in Jonah's repertoire.

While inside the belly of the great fish, Jonah spoke powerful words of God's faithfulness to him. As he awaited his own personal redemption, he remembered his God, and pledged to be faithful again in Jonah 2:8-9:

*"Those who cling to worthless idols
  turn away from God's love for them.
But I, with shouts of grateful praise,
  will sacrifice to You.
What I have vowed I will make good.
  I will say, 'Salvation comes from the Lord.'"*

The book of Jonah shows that God deals with our shortcomings, even if they are "on paper." God revealed a different side of Himself to Jonah, resulting in a long-lasting lesson and experience of faithfulness. God was teaching Jonah, above all things, about the need to be faithful.

Faithfulness and idolatry

In keeping with what we just discussed, faithfulness and idolatry are inseparable when it comes to our relationship with God and understanding what it means to be faithful. We serve a God Who is worthy of our worship and devotion. We cannot serve two masters at once (Matthew 6:24, Luke 16:13). Our personal sense of order must submit to the true God and His precepts. Everything else leads us astray, into a place of idolatry.

This is another place where faithfulness often causes us discomfort. None of us look around our lives and immediately see the things we've created as idols. We think idols are small statues, things seen in pagan religions (or perhaps Catholicism), but never the wonders of our own lives. We are bereft to admit that anything can be an idol, and sometimes the idols of our own doing are the closest "sacred cows" we can find.

Faithfulness is a matter of both focus and commitment. Before any relationship we have in this life, we must learn to be faithful in our relationship with God. In that, our relationship with God needs to be the pursuit of God Himself, not the benefits of it, our own obvious works, and not what we get out of it, but a sincere pursuit of God, for the sacred majesty that He is.

To repeat: faithfulness pursues God. Not the miracle. Not the breakthrough. Not the salvation of all your unsaved family members. It's being more committed to God than expecting God to "prove Himself" when you have a need. Faithfulness keeps God first in every aspect of life, whether things are good, or things are hard.

We are quick to quote Joshua 24:15, but Joshua 24:14 lays the groundwork for properly understanding that verse:

"Now fear the LORD and serve Him with all faithfulness. Throw away the gods your ancestors worshiped beyond the Euphrates River and in Egypt, and serve the LORD. But if serving the LORD seems undesirable to you, then choose for yourselves this day whom you will serve, whether the gods your ancestors served beyond the Euphrates, or the gods of the Amorites, in whose land you are living. But as for me and my household, we will serve the LORD."

We are encouraged to serve God without any question, hesitation, or second thoughts. If we have those second thoughts, we need to deal with them and move past them. If we say that we believe in God and have faith in Him, then that means being faithful in every way possible and in every concept...even beyond believing Him just for what He can do.

Relationships require faithfulness

As I prepared to write this chapter, God pointed out that we want to pray and talk about marriages today: left, right, and sideways. They are used as political fodder and are a general topic for most ministries. Marriages are lamented, treated as if they will one day be no more, and we are constantly told to pray for them. What we don't pray for – or teach on – to help marriages is an understanding of faithfulness. In fact, we don't seem to recognize that if faithfulness is lacking in any relationship of any sort, the relationship is doomed to failure.

Amos 3:3:

Do two walk together
unless they have agreed to do so?

Agreement is a powerful thing in a relationship. We find agreement through faithfulness. It's easy to think divorced couples didn't try hard enough and wayward friends or family members were just casualties. The majority of the time, faithfulness was, in some way or another, an issue in that relationship. There are many ways relationships require faithfulness:

> **FOUNDATIONAL FERTILIZER:** The early years of ministry are often very difficult for the ambitious minister who has seen the end of their ministry work, rather than the beginning. When people ask me what my secret is to being in ministry all these years, my simple answer is that I was faithfully persistent in moving through those early years, on to better years. If you are in the early years of ministry, the only secret to making it through is consistent faithfulness.

- **Marriage/dating**: I know some reading this will take issue with coupling marriage and dating together in the area of faithfulness, but the truth is that dating is training for the kind of relationship one wants to have long-term. This means faithfulness is required in dating and marriage relationships in the same way. It's understood that if a relationship is serious, neither partner is seeing other people, they are committed to the relationship, and they are committed to work out differences and, ultimately, to one another. Faithfulness starts long before affairs ever enter a picture and is relevant even if neither partner is having or has had an affair. Faithfulness manifests in encouragement, in supporting the other partner in their dreams and life desires, and in the commitment to accept that person as they are, good points, flaws and all.

- **Friendships**: Friendships are built on faithfulness, because they are built on the promise to be there for one other, no matter how difficult things may be. Friends choose faithfulness, especially when they can't rely on others to be there for them.

- **Parents and children**: Parents must be faithful to the care and nurturing of their children to raise them well. While there's no question that even parents who do their best make mistakes, faithfulness is a necessity for the day-in, day-out demands of parenthood. Parenting is not just a fly-by-night endeavor where children are born and left to their own devices. Being a parent means being in the work for the long-haul: when kids are cute, not so cute, downright spiteful in adolescence, and there for them when they need you as adults. It is understood that as parents try to care for their children, children will be faithful to parents in the form of obedience and respect.

- **Ministers and congregations**: Leaders are worthy of double honor (1 Timothy 5:17) because they do double the work. This takes faithfulness to God, the work and the vision, and to everyone they are called to lead and care for within God's grace. Those who are a part of a congregation or who are covered by a leader are expected to be faithful to that leader in tithes and offerings, attendance, dedication to learning about worship, Scripture, and practical Christian living, and participation.

- **Leaders and members**: Everyone in church is required to be both faithful and accountable to someone else. Ideally, we learn from this foundational relationship how to be faithful and accountable to the entire Body of Christ. Leaders should still have other leaders, and should be faithful and trustworthy members as a part of that leader's ministry. Leaders who lead other leaders, in turn, should be faithful to those they lead, remaining faithful to them even in difficult times.

Faith without works…

Let's face it: nobody's favorite Bible verse is found in James 2. Historically speaking, some of the most famous figures of faith in history wanted to disregard the book of James because its contents are…well…convicting. This conviction that feels oh-so-not-good has caused James 2 to be of considerable debate over the years, causing confusion as to just what our relationship with works should be. People want to push the conviction away, convince themselves that they are "good enough" as they are because they have Jesus, and leave it at that.

That conviction we feel is the Holy Spirit working within us, calling us to a greater faithfulness in our lives. We keep trying to shut it out in the hopes that it'll go away, but the call to faithfulness is for all of us. If we want to be faithful, we need to hear the words spoken in James 2:14-26, loud and clear:

What good is it, my brothers and sisters, if someone claims to have faith but has no deeds? Can such faith save them? Suppose a brother or sister is without clothes and daily food. If one of you says to them, "Go, in peace; keep warm and well fed," but does nothing about their physical needs, what good is it? In the same way, faith by itself, if it is not accompanied by action, is dead.

But someone will say, "You have faith; I have deeds."

Show me your faith without deeds, and I will show you my faith by my deeds. You believe that there is one God. Good! Even the demons believe that — and shudder.

You foolish person, do you want evidence that faith without deeds is useless? Was not our father Abraham considered righteous for what he did when he offered his son Isaac on the altar? You see that his faith and his actions were working together, and his faith was made complete by what he did. And the Scripture was fulfilled that says, "Abraham believed God, and it was credited to him as righteousness," and he was called God's friend. You see that a person is considered righteous by what they do and not by faith alone.

> **HAPPY HARVEST:** If you are forgetful of things, keep a datebook or calendar to help you remember the commitments you've made. This will help you be more faithful to them.

In the same way, was not even Rahab the prostitute considered righteous for what she did when she gave lodging to the spies and sent them off in a different direction? As the body without the spirit is dead, so faith without deeds is dead.

Faith without works is still dead! It doesn't mean they save us, or that we save ourselves by them, but that the work of faith in our lives is shown through our faithful commitments to God and to others. If faith without works is dead, that means faithfulness is alive! It is what keeps us alive and keeps our faith active and vibrant. Any time our walk with God starts to get stagnant, it is because we are not being faithful enough to the call we have in Him.

Our call to follow God in faithfulness is not about us being "good enough." It's not about us reading these stories of people in Scripture, such as Abraham, and looking at their deeds to feel like we will never be as good as we should be. On the contrary, God doesn't ask us to be as good as anyone else. Even people in the Bible had their personal faults, failings, and mistakes. Every single one of them was human. They all had one thing in common, though, and that was their commitment to display their faith through their works, unto the walk and work of faithfulness. No matter how hard it may be or seem, we are still called to this same level of faithfulness today. It is just as obtainable through the Spirit as it was back then.

Keeping our word and our commitments

I used to remember everything without a datebook: every single appointment, commitment, promise to call someone back, preaching engagements, lunch dates, counseling sessions, book releases, and every other single detail of my life. The first time I realized I forgot something was when I was asked to write for an e-zine. Because no one got back to me about the project, the deadline for the event came and went. I still didn't start using my datebook like I should have, and I would go on to forget many other things from time to time. Even though they might not have been huge opportunities or matters, it still bothered me that I forgot anything at all. I knew that if I wanted to be somebody who was of good reputation in ministry, I needed to be faithful, and that meant keeping my word and my commitments.

We all have moments where we genuinely forget things, lapse in our thoughts, or are unable to follow through on something because we have emergencies or issues that demand our immediate or full attention. However, this isn't the case on a regular basis. If we look over church today, people say they will do things all the time, and then they do not show up. They commit to be somewhere, and then don't follow through. These are signs that they lack faithfulness.

God expects those who call themselves by His Name to be faithful people, keeping our word and seeing our commitments through to the end. As it says in Ecclesiastes 5:4-7:

When you make a vow to God, do not delay to fulfill it. He has no pleasure in fools; fulfill your vow. It is better not to vow than to make one and not fulfill it. Do not let your mouth lead you into sin. And do not protest to the temple messenger, "My vow was a mistake." Why should God be angry at what you say and destroy the work of your hands? Much dreaming and many words are meaningless. Therefore fear God.

This verse brings us full circle, back to the original issues we discussed and every other issue we've considered throughout this chapter. Faithfulness is a characteristic of the way we live our lives. It means we keep our word, we do right by others, and ultimately, that we live our faith. I pray we will start seeing more faithfulness in the church in our times.

Producing more excellent fruit

Where are you when it comes to faithfulness? Where can you do better? Here are some suggestions on ways to produce a more excellent fruit of faithfulness:

- **Study more about faithfulness, especially looking at people in the Bible**: Contrary to the way we have idolized them, Bible people were far from perfect. They were everyday people, living everyday lives, who were faithful to the things God asked of them. (In fact, the Bible also shows what happened to people who were not faithful to God, as well!) In reading about these people, see them as people rather than as super-holy, super-spiritual beings. Then, see yourself. From here, look at ways you can be more dedicated and faithful in your own life.

- **Be more involved at church**: I have yet to visit a church that is not hurting for faithful volunteers or attendees. We talked in the chapter on goodness about being faithful with tithes and offerings, but most ministries need help that goes beyond the financial. It is a struggle to get people to offer to help with Sunday School, nursery, clean-up, decoration, hospitality, and altar work, because these things are deemed to be "demeaning" by modern standards. If you want to develop a faithful fruit, find something your church needs help with, and faithfully assist with that need.

- **Don't make promises you can't keep**: If your calendar is brimming with dates, events, things to attend, and help with, you are going to start forgetting things. If you know beyond a shadow of a doubt that you really don't have time for something else in your life right now, then say that, rather than pledging to be somewhere or do something that you won't be able to do.

- **Pray with others**: Praying by ourselves is great, but praying with others offers a power-packed session that we should never cut out, nor eliminate, from our lives. Gathering in small groups is an awesome way to set up accountability and faithfulness as you pray for and strive with others who also walk through the ins and outs of faith.

- **Talk out a problem with someone you are close to instead of sulking and cutting them out of your life**: I need to start off by saying that some people need to be cut out of your life. I am not an advocate that we should keep everyone around all the time. I think whether someone needs to go is a discernment call, and I am in no way contradicting that discernment process. Now that I said that sometimes we are hasty to cut people out of our lives because we don't want to deal with the disciplines of being in relationship with that person (i.e., we don't want to be faithful with them). They take too much time, talk too much, demand too much, want too much, etc., and in all these generalizations (that may or may not be true), we forget the reason we wanted them in our lives in the first place. Instead of running, talk out some problems (at least give it a try) and see where things take you.

- **Reject false teachers**: False teachers don't always come around talking about aliens and space monkeys. Most false teachers say things that appeal to us in many ways (i.e., the parts of us that want faithfulness and God-oriented things to be easy). No matter how nice it might sound...no matter how comfy it might be…no matter how entertaining they may be…reject false teachers, because they turn us away from faithfulness.

- **Consider your interpersonal influences**: I'm not one of those preachers that think for you to be a Christian, you must forsake everyone in your life who is not. I know many people who aren't Christian, and I also know many members of my church have non-Christian friends, as well. We stand as ensigns to God's love in their lives, and this is as important and essential as anything else. Saying Christians shouldn't have non-Christian friends is too general and sends the message that Christians are always perfect (when they are not) and that Christians are a better influence on other Christians (this is not always the case). At the same time, we should consider who is around us. Are our friends, influences, leaders, etc. encouraging us to be faithful in our walk with God? If you are around people who don't respect your relationship with God, you are around the wrong people…no matter what they espouse for doctrine on paper.

Chapter Nine

Gentleness (Humility)

Those who disregard discipline despise themselves,
but the one who heeds correction gains understanding.
Wisdom's instruction is to fear the Lord,
and humility comes before honor.
- Proverbs 15:32-33

Assignments:
- Read Colossians 3:12-17.
- Monitor your speech for five days and make a point to speak with respect and grace when interacting with others.
- Let someone else go first, for a change.

For almost ten years, I was the owner of two dogs, both yellow Labrador Retrievers. One was male (Gideon), and one was female (Fiona). They were both wonderful dogs, but the two couldn't have been more different in their personalities. Gideon was extremely gentle, while Fiona was like a bull in a China shop. It was fascinating to watch the two of them throughout the duration of their lives (Fiona lived to be ten, while Gideon lived to be almost 15). When Fiona was alive, Gideon always stepped aside, so as not to compete with Fiona, who was always everywhere, in everything. When I'd try to give Fiona a treat, she bit my hand a few times to get it (it wasn't deliberate, but she was that into the whole scene). Gideon was so gentle, it was as if you were feeding a deer from your hand. He always let her step back and eat ravenously, waiting for someone to give him something directly. When he was ready to go out in the morning, he'd gently lick someone's face and nudge them with his snout, while Fiona would roll around on the floor and kick around until she woke you up!

I know from watching them for so many years that Gideon got tired of having to step aside and give Fiona the space she claimed for herself. After she died from complications related to Cushing's Syndrome, he was relieved to spend another four years with his own food, treats, attention, and time, as he no longer had to compete with her. Still, Gideon was always loved for his sweet, soft nature. He always received lots of love and attention from those who met him, because they appreciated his unique nature. Nobody ever met Gideon and didn't think he was the best tempered dog they every met.

Fiona was also deeply loved and appreciated for who she was.

We loved her boldness, her feistiness, and her spunky nature. Still, I can't deny, even today, that the way she carried herself wasn't always beneficial. Her relationship with Gideon would have been better if she had restrained herself a bit. As much as she loved people, she often came on very strong and intimidating, and not everyone responded to her in the way she might have liked. I know now that she had a disorder that drove her to both eat and interact a bit compulsively, and that she couldn't help herself. But if she'd been a little gentler in her countenance, it might have helped her interactions with others throughout her life.

We live in a hostile, aggressive world that encourages people to behave more like Fiona than Gideon. We are taught that the more aggressive we are, the better we are. Go-getter attitudes are considered an attribute. We are encouraged to squash competition, edge other people out, and push, push, push to get our way and our agenda across. Funny how the Bible encourages us to be the opposite: quiet, humble, meek, and yes, gentle. The Bible doesn't tell us to morph into different people (I, for one, have a voice that often carries), but it tells us to be conscious of how we carry ourselves. Even though aggression might get us something we want in the immediate, in the long run, it alienates us from others. If we are to be effective Gospel messengers, engaging when we take on and tackle spiritual things, and those who desire to grow in God, we must remove aggression and put on a garment of gentleness.

What is gentleness?

Gentleness is the condition or countenance of being gentle. It is in contrast with being harsh or overbearing. The term is found exclusively in the New Testament, a total of six times. The principle of gentleness, however, is found far more than just six times in Scripture. Throughout the Bible, we are encouraged to exercise meekness and mildness, to answer others softly, and to avoid aggressive confrontation.

1 Timothy 6:3-16:

If anyone teaches otherwise and does not agree to the sound instruction of our

Lord Jesus Christ and to godly teaching, they are conceited and understand nothing. They have an unhealthy interest in controversies and quarrels about words that result in envy, strife, malicious talk, evil suspicions and constant friction between people of corrupt mind, who have been robbed of the truth and who think that godliness is a means to financial gain.

But godliness with contentment is great gain. For we brought nothing into the world, and we can take nothing out of it. But if we have food and clothing, we will be content with that. Those who want to get rich fall into temptation and a trap and into many foolish and harmful desires that plunge people into ruin and destruction. For the love of money is a root of all kinds of evil. Some people, eager for money, have wandered from the faith and pierced themselves with many griefs.

> **BUD BREAKS:**
> **Gentleness** #4236
> *praotes* [prah-ot'-ace]:
> gentleness, mildness, meekness.

But you, man of God, flee from all this, and pursue righteousness, godliness, faith, love, endurance and gentleness. Fight the good fight of the faith. Take hold of the eternal life to which you were called when you made your good confession in the presence of many witnesses. In the sight of God, Who gives life to everything, and of Christ Jesus, Who while testifying before Pontius Pilate made the good confession, I charge you to keep this command without spot or blame until the appearing of our Lord Jesus Christ, which God will bring about in His own time – God, the blessed and only Ruler, the King of kings and Lord of lords, Who alone is immortal and Who lives in unapproachable light, Whom no one has seen or can see. To Him be honor and might forever. Amen.

- **Gentleness listens to true doctrine and sound instruction**: Gentleness can sit still long enough to listen to what is true and consider it, as well as live by it. Those who are abrasive are unable to listen and are unable to receive truth, because they are too busy trying to defend what they already think. As a side point: gentleness listens because it doesn't have to have the last word. It considers where it might be wrong, and grows in the grace to accept truth, no matter how it comes.

- **Gentleness is not conceited, nor vague in understanding**: Arrogance is extremely unattractive. It comes in and demands its way, all because it is there. When someone is gentle, they are not conceited. They can be taught as needed, and therefore never lack understanding. Gentle people are eager to learn, eager to know more, and are willing to listen to perspectives so as to gain an even better sense of understanding in all situations.

- **Gentleness does not take interest in controversies and quarrels (or their results)**: We've discussed more than one fruit that advises against engaging in needless controversies and quarrels. We all know that some like to fight and argue for no good reason at all, and some are determined to provoke those arguments for no other purpose except to argue. If you truly have and walk in the truth, you don't need to fight with everyone, nor state your claim all the time. Gentleness provides the confidence to sit back and avoid needless arguments. There's no pursuit to be right or have the last word in every situation.

- **Gentleness operates with contentment for great gain**: Contentment is an important principle in the Christian life. While the world seeks after ambitions, objects, and desires that never seem to satisfy, gentleness adopts the principle that in all things, I can be content. It's fine to have goals and to desire to do things in life, but gentleness proves that things do not make us content…we are content when we are satisfied because we have God in our lives.

- **Gentleness does not love money**: The passage above states that the love of money leads to a piercing with many sorrows. Why is this? If we always seek money as the answer to every issue, we will never be content. If capitalism serves as a lesson to us about money, it never seems as if enough is enough. The more we have, the more we want, and still the more we seek after that. In gentle contentment, we don't love money, we love God. Whatever we have, we trust that God will provide for us.

- **Gentleness operates with righteousness, godliness, faith, love, and endurance**: I mention this because so many of these things are either mentioned earlier in the fruit of the Spirit or relate to the fruit of the Spirit. Becoming a gentle person doesn't start and end with a desire to be nice. It functions as we seek to be righteous, godly, faithful, loving, and enduring (patient)!

- **Gentleness helps us fight the good fight of faith**: Athletes know that giving their all right away in a sprint, sporting event, or other athletic pursuit is a mistake. They wind up exhausted and, ultimately, losing their race, game, or sport. Good athletes are taught to pace themselves, exercising good judgment to endure for the duration. Games, races, and athletic pursuits are won by strategy. Gentleness is the strategy to helps us fight the good fight of faith, even after years of exhaustion. Gentleness helps us to pace ourselves.

The decorative fixtures of our spiritual house

I compare gentleness to the decorations of a house. Decorative fixtures are the "finishing touches" in a home, accenting any existing design. Fixtures in a home are typically a matter of individual tastes: some like brass or nickel fixtures, some like copper, some like paintings, others are into statues or figurines, some like mirrors, some like carpeting, others like wood floors…I am sure you can get the picture. Gentleness operates in much of the same way. It is a "finishing touch" on our character, on the way we choose to live our lives and how we choose to interact with other people. It doesn't change who we are, but it adds to it, allowing us to stand ready and compliment everything we do.

Attributes of gentleness

I'm sure some of you are wondering how gentleness can work for everyone. Why does the Bible list gentleness specifically in connection with the fruit of the Spirit? Surely everyone is not gentle, right? Some people are just "brawny" and aggressive by their very nature. Gentleness can't be for everyone…can it?

If there was anyone who did not have a natural inclination toward gentleness, it was the Apostle Paul. I believe this is why he is the author of five New Testament references to gentleness (the other one being the Apostle Peter, who was also not gentle in his natural temperament). Paul had to work at being gentle. It came up more than once in his writings because he too needed the reminder, recognizing others needed it, as well. From what we know about Paul before his conversion to Christianity, he was a punitive murderer, aggressive, quick-tempered, frequently angry, quick to have others killed, and believed his way was the correct way in all matters. Gentleness wasn't a consideration! He would have seen the concept as an area of weakness. Jesus had to personally appear to him and knock him off his high horse to get him to see that, no matter how right he might have felt about his way of life and living, he wasn't the person he was called to be.

If Paul (and also Peter) could write on gentleness and develop it in their lives, the rest of us can, too. It's never too late to develop more attributes of the fruit of the Spirit. Goodness is no exception to the spiritual rule! So, those with bad tempers, harsh attitudes, aggressive tendencies, issues with pride, annoyed countenances, and the like unite and dedicate yourselves to learning more about the fruit of gentleness!

Colossians 3:12-17 says:

Therefore, as God's chosen people, holy and dearly loved, clothe yourselves with compassion, kindness, humility, gentleness and patience. Bear with each other and forgive one another if any of you has a grievance against someone. Forgive as the Lord forgave you. And over all these virtues put on love, which binds them all together in perfect unity.

Let the peace of Christ rule in your hearts, since as members of one body you were called to peace. And be thankful. Let the word of Christ dwell among you richly as you teach and admonish one another with all wisdom through psalms, hymns and songs from the Spirit, singing to God with gratitude in your hearts. And whatever you do, whether in word or deed, do it all in the Name of the Lord Jesus, giving thanks to God the Father through Him.

It's not an accident that contentment comes up, yet again, in connection with gentleness. We can see in this passage that the Apostle Paul equated gentle behavior with contentment. Is there something more to this that we should think about? I believe so. This passage in Colossians 3 speaks of contentment with one another, the result of which is the ability to be gentle. In gentleness, we are called to clothe – as in, put on these things that may not always come along with our nature – compassion, kindness, humility, gentleness, and patience. As a command, we put them on, just as if we are putting on clothes or shoes. We aren't born wearing clothes. Sometimes the outfit fits, sometimes it doesn't, and sometimes we need to change it. Here we are urged to change our spiritual garment so that it fits the royal garments of our King. In so doing, we adapt – put on – the fruit of gentleness.

> **PRUNING POINTS:** I am not opposed to the use of titles in church. Titles help us identify work as we define terms. It also helps us acknowledge those who walk in those offices. However, we can learn something from John the Baptist in this regard. He refused to take on a role that others tried to assign to him in the name of defining their own concepts of a spiritual work. I've met many people who wanted to be an apostle or a prophet because of how it looks to them from the outside, according to what they have seen other people do in it or with it. Instead of looking at what humans create, listen to God and learn what He wants to develop within you. Desiring offices because they look some way on the outside is the surest way to enter ministry for the wrong reasons.

Also essential to gentleness is forgiveness. Yes, this applies in situations where it's most necessary – when we have a grievance with someone else. Gentleness considers not just the desire of contentment, but the condition of it. If we are to find contentment in life, we must be people who forgive. When we don't forgive, we carry around anger and hostility, spending life either actively or passively aggressive. This leads to frustration, especially over past matters that we can't go back and change. Gentleness recognizes the importance of living now, in this moment, and embracing others in love (especially the community of believers). Instead of dwelling on what we can't change, we focus on living as God calls us to live. There's a freedom in this, one that leads us to victory in many areas of life.

In gentleness, we let our inner joy shine forth. We can teach one another and receive sound teaching, accepting word and instruction as it's given. We receive it as it's given: in a gentle and right spirit. We sing the songs of praise and worship, feeling grateful for all God has given us and for all He does for us. Because nothing we do is contrary to Christ, we are able to do all in His Name. Gentleness is a virtue that changes us and, by proxy, also changes the church. When we operate gentleness, our conduct is clear and known before all.

Gentleness and humility

In some translations of the Bible, the term "gentleness" is translated as "humility." What is interesting about this is that the word "humility" is not actually found anywhere in the definition we have of the Greek word, *praotes*. I understand what the translators were trying to do, and in keeping with that, I believe gentleness and humility are connected. Gentleness is the countenance, or composure, that humility brings. Every one of us has dealt with someone who was arrogant and conceited. They carry themselves in a certain manner that is not only off-putting, but makes others feel like they should be subordinate to them. As a result, nobody wants to be around them. Humility, or the ability to maintain a certain amount of modesty when it comes to one's own importance, is something that allows the work of gentleness to flow. If we don't need others to constantly pay attention to us or to pay us some sort of generalized honor (that is often undeserved), we are able to focus on other things, on things outside of ourselves that lead us to a place of deeper contentment and spiritual focus.

The Bible tells us the greatest prophet up until New Testament times was John the Baptist (Matthew 11:11). Even though John was vitally important in salvation history, he walked in a state of intense humility throughout his life. He was, after all, the baptizer to end all baptizers! People came from all around to hear him preach against sin and be baptized by him in the Jordan River. Surely, he had reason to get a big, swollen head, but he didn't get one. When confronted with Jesus in John 1:19-27, John's response is most interesting:

Now this was John's testimony when the Jewish leaders in Jerusalem sent priests and Levites to ask him who he was. He did not fail to confess, but confessed freely, "I am not the Christ."

They asked him, "Then who are you? Are you Elijah?"

He said, "I am not."

"Are you a prophet?"

He answered, "No."

Finally they said, "Who are you? Give us an answer to take back to those who sent us. What do you say about yourself?"

John replied in the words of Isaiah the prophet, "I am the voice of one calling in the desert, 'Make straight the way for the Lord.'"

Now some Pharisees who had been sent questioned him, "Why then do you baptize if you are not the Messiah, nor Elijah, nor the Prophet?"

"I baptize with water," John replied, "but among you stands One you do not know. He is the One Who comes after me, the straps of whose sandals I am not worthy to untie."

Fully well knowing his assignment, John the Baptist didn't even consider himself a prophet! He was doing what God asked him to do. His focus wasn't on defining himself for others but on preparing the way for Christ to come. This led him to be gentle in his reply, and gentle in the way he handled baptism as those came with repentant hearts to be baptized in preparation for the coming of the Messiah.

Humility enables us to be gentle. Gentleness ensures we will remain humble. The two together promise us that we will walk in a place of contentment.

"You can catch more flies with honey than with vinegar!"

One of my mom's "old sayings" is, "You can catch more flies with honey than with vinegar!" Because I was born in an era of fly swatters and bug zappers, I found this expression to be quite questionable as a child. Nobody put out bowls of honey or vinegar in the hopes of catching a bunch of flies. From what I understand about the English proverb, it goes back beyond the *Poor Richard's Almanac* (1744) to an Italian book of proverbs published sometime way before 1744. In other words, the expression's contents, in one form or another, go back quite far. I would imagine that before the days of bug spray, people probably did try various home remedies to try and control pests in their homes. It does make sense that someone noticed honey's sticky consistency and thought, "I know, let's see if I can catch some flies with this!" Then someone else, thinking that vinegar is fermented fruit, also put some out, and tried a little experiment themselves. While it might have killed the insects, it didn't attract them.

We now know the expression to mean that you can get much farther with others if you are gentle with them rather than being acidic or nasty. In terms of gentleness, this expression has a lot to offer. All of us remember "church mothers" (or in my case growing up, nuns) who were older women in the church that sought to instill values and guidance within younger members of the church. Personally, I think the older women working with the younger women is a great and Biblical idea (Titus 2:4). The problem with memories of "church mothers" is that most people don't have many positive experiences to share about them. Most people who talk about these women speak of them as harsh and critical, picking at little things in young women's attire and appearance, cussing at them, and fussing with things as pertain to their futures and personal lives. Most of who have spoken to me about the role of church mothers describe them as being downright mean and nasty. All those who described church mothers in this way also went their own way, often leaving church for a period of time and living in ways that the church mothers most definitely would have disagreed with in one fashion or another.

I understand that people of past generations often had different standards of conduct and character than we do today. Many thought being hard on youth was a good idea, as it would help them develop character. I also would say that when it came to advice, church mothers weren't always wrong. But I can't help but think that if the church mothers had adopted a principle of gentleness, expressing this essential fruit of the Spirit among young members of the church, the outcome of some situations might have been markedly different. If, instead of picking on youth the church mothers had encouraged them to pursue education and careers, learn they are more than a sex object, and listened to their thoughts and feelings about growing up without blowing them off, maybe some of these youths would have felt there was more for them in church than being the target of angry taunts. The Bible encourages us to be gentle and develop

> **FOUNDATIONAL FERTILIZER:** Being young is hard enough. Youth deal with temptations, trials, and confusion as they try to sort out things for themselves. In my own life, I had my share of "church mothers" who, although did not go by that title, behaved much in the way that others tell me church mothers behave. They planned my future for me, criticized my clothing, pulled me in many different directions, and caused me such confusion, I stopped listening to them all together. When guiding young people, keep in mind that they are not living your life. They have their own life to live and need gentle guidance to live that life, not your own.

gentleness because it makes others know they can trust us, especially when things come up that are sensitive or personal in nature. Gentleness lets others know we won't judge or criticize them. This is more important than it might sound, especially given many believe judgment is akin to godliness. (Hint: it's not.)

Proverbs 15:1-2:

A gentle answer turns away wrath,
   but a harsh word stirs up anger.

The tongue of the wise adorns knowledge,
   but the mouth of the fool gushes folly.

> **POLLINATION POWER:** Do you desire to teach others? If so, take to heart the words of James 3:1-12! Those who teach are judged not just for what they casually say, but for what they teach other people! If you want to teach, make sure you embody the spirit of gentleness!

We can use any excuses we like to keep various traditions alive, defending them in the name of "holiness." If we are all willing to step back and look at our own experiences, we can all testify to one point: we are more apt to present truth if it's presented to us in a gentle fashion. If we receive harsh words, we are more likely to be defensive and reject them. Gentleness reminds us that the way we speak to others matters. We should always speak to others in the way we would like others to speak to us. Holiness doesn't mean being rash or crude, but set apart with the necessary insights to transform the world on God's terms. One of His terms is, you guessed it – gentleness.

Taming the tongue

If we want to see the principle of gentleness work in our lives, we must consider the relevance of taming the tongue. In the example I gave of church mothers, they were not women out rousing the streets with alcohol or wildly engaging in different sexual practices. Such was against their beliefs. To them, to do such things would have been a disgrace. No matter what they did when they were younger, they were past the point of deliberately "sinning" in their lives. They were not women, however, who were trained to tame their tongues. They got the connection between actions and belief, but not words and countenance. The result of such had its own complications and detriments.

All of us – I repeat, every single one of us – needs to develop the discipline of the tongue. Remember in the last chapter I said that nobody's favorite Bible verse is found in James chapter 2? Well, I am really going to venture that the same is true for James chapter 3. None of us like to hear or think that maybe the way we talk to others is wrong or that maybe we need to discipline our speech as much as we discipline any other area of our physical and spiritual selves. If we will be gentle people, we need to take the words about the tongue to heart, especially to remain in focus for gentle speech. James 3:1-12 says:

Not many of you should presume to be teachers, my fellow believers, because you know that we who teach will be judged more strictly. We all stumble in many ways. Anyone who is never at fault in what they say is perfect, able to keep their whole body in check.

When we put bits into the mouths of horses to make them obey us, we can turn the whole animal. Or take ships as an example. Although they are so large and are driven by strong winds, they are steered by a very small rudder wherever the pilot wants to go. Likewise, the tongue is a small part of the body, but it makes great boasts. Consider what a great forest is set on fire by a small spark. The tongue also is a fire, a world of evil among the parts of the body. It corrupts the whole body, sets the whole course of one's life on fire, and is itself set on fire by hell.

All kinds of animals, birds, reptiles and creatures of the sea are being tamed and have been tamed by mankind, but no man can tame the tongue. It is a restless evil, full of deadly poison.

With the tongue we praise our Lord and Father, and with it we curse human beings, who have been made in God's likeness. Out of the same mouth come praising and cursing. My brothers and sisters, this should not be. Can both fresh water and salt water flow from the same spring? My brothers, can a fig tree bear olives, or a grapevine bear figs? Neither can a salt spring produce fresh water.

These words on the tongue give some important food for thought when it comes to speech. James clarifies that it is very, very difficult for us to tame our tongues. It seems easier to tame an entire animal than it is to control what we say! Difficult as it may be, it is very, very important we do so, especially if we want to be in ministry or in a position to teach others. What he is telling us, bottom line, is that what we say matters. We can either approach people in a gentle spirit, or we can come at them in a manner that is unbecoming and will be rejected automatically, no matter what we have to say.

1 Peter 3:13-16:

> **HAPPY HARVEST:** Who would you consider to be a model of gentleness in your life? Think of some ways you can emulate some of their characteristics in your own life.

Who is going to harm you if you are eager to do good? But even if you should suffer for what is right, you are blessed. "Do not fear their threats; do not be frightened." But in your hearts revere Christ as Lord. Always be prepared to give an answer to everyone who asks you to give the reason for the hope that you have. But do this with gentleness and respect, keeping a clear conscience, so that those who speak maliciously against your good behavior in Christ may be ashamed of their slander.

We touched on this verse in an earlier chapter, but I want to touch on it again. This time, we will look at it in connection with gentleness. The Apostle Peter's words echo those of James, even though they were not written about the same thing. Gentleness is not about walking into a room in silence or wearing dull colors all the time. It is about how we interact, and in large part, how we speak to and treat other people. If we are not content with our own lives and where we are at with God, we are going to behave in ways that are intolerant and harsh with others. Why is this? Because we are resentful and angry of how we feel "God" is forcing us to be. God has never, at any point in the Scriptures, told us we can't be people of joy (quite the opposite, in fact), or ever have a good time or enjoy anything. We aren't called to be uptight people who look like we swallowed a coat hanger. If we aren't content with Him, we aren't going to find gentleness in our interactions with others. Wherever you lack contentment, it's time to grow past it and gain deeper understanding about where you find yourself in life. If you adopt the fruit of gentleness, you will be gentle, and those who seek to destroy you and, by extension, the church, will be silenced.

The meek shall inherit...

In writing this final section for this chapter, it's important to mention the term "gentleness" can also be translated as "meekness." While the term "meek" is not found in the Bible very much (four times, three of which are in the Old Testament and one is in the New), it is found in one very powerful and important passage which further confirms for us about the call and command to be gentle.

Being meek is the equivalent of being gentle, in that it is a countenance that embodies humility and contentment. It isn't trying to outdo anyone else or compete with anyone else; it allows others to be who they are and is content with who or what it is. Contrary to worldly pop culture, being meek doesn't mean being timid, nor does it mean being weak. It gives people the space to be themselves, with respect and gentleness, and maintains inner contentment at the same time. Meekness is a place of balance, one that reflects the best of heaven down here on earth, handling the difficulties of holiness and individuality at the same time.

In one of Jesus' most famous sermons, He makes the following statement about the meek in Matthew 5:5:

Blessed are the meek,
for they will inherit the earth.

Jesus promises that those who were meek – who are humble and gentle – will receive the goodness of the land. Rather than it just being limited to one nation or location, He promised the meek all the land, the entire earth. This is incredible to fathom, because Jesus tells those who embody the virtue of gentleness that, one day, all of this (everything conceivable) will be theirs.

There's a bigger promise in here that we must be sure not to miss. Meekness will be, at some point in the future, a fully rewardable and desirable characteristic. Harshness, violence, and arrogance will, one day, cease. Gentleness will have at its fullness the attention of all the world's inhabitants. In other words, the world as we know it won't last forever. The seemingly mighty, strong, and all-powerful powers that be won't have power forever. Whatever they did to ascend to power will no longer matter, and no one will desire their characteristics anymore. Meekness, humility, and gentleness will reign, and the result will be world peace.

Even though we know the world is at odds with the church, the church should see itself as a part of the inheritance of the gentle. As the Kingdom of God this side of heaven, gentleness should take front and center stage among believers who know that Jesus has called them to conduct themselves in a manner that's reward rests in the inheritance of the earth. Rather than advocating crude or aggressive forms of church life, we should all uphold the precepts He taught…with gentleness…in the same manner that He Himself also taught them.

Producing more excellent fruit

Where are you when it comes to gentleness? Where can you do better? Here are some suggestions on ways to produce a more excellent fruit of gentleness:

- **Take a second (or third, or tenth) look at the Beatitudes**: The Beatitudes, as we call them, are found in Matthew 5:1-12. They speak of specific groups of people and the blessing they receive as a part of who they are and the characteristics they reflect. As discussed in the last section, "meekness" (a form of gentleness) is specifically mentioned in the Beatitudes. The Beatitudes tell us a lot about living in gentle ways and about embodying lifestyles of gentleness. In a hostile world, the Beatitudes are worth a study through the eyes of gentleness.

- **Stop trying to change other people**: It's hard to watch others take a course that you disagree with, or you feel will, in some way, be harmful to them or others. Arguing, nagging, and debating isn't going to change what they do. If anything, it might make their course seem more appealing. Instead of trying to change others, be there for them. You are welcome to state your disagreement but do it with gentleness. Through your interactions, let them know that no matter what happens, you will be there for them and love them. No matter how much you yell, scream, and nag, you are not going to be able to change anyone.

- **Keep track of how you talk to others**: We could go on and on about speech and words and about how we speak in general, but it's important to look specifically at how we speak to one another. I've heard of people adopting the idea of a "swear jar," where every time they use profanity, they put in a quarter or a dime or some small denomination and then give the entire amount to charity. Instead of doing it with profanity, start a "gentle speech" jar and put in money every time you interact with someone, and the course of discussion could be described as coarse, harsh, or unflattering. At the end of the month, take the money and give it to charity.

- **Think before you speak!**: Continuing the idea of keeping track of how you speak to others, think about what you are going to say before you say it. If it doesn't sound right in your head or you would be offended if someone said it to you, maybe you need to re-think how you can word it, or for the time being, not say anything at all.

- **Smile more!**: I am a rather serious person by nature. I don't smile much, especially when I am thinking (I'm seeing where my thoughts take me. A lot of what I see, deal with, and consider in a day is serious and sometimes unpleasant. Smiling has a way of lifting my spirits and opening up the door for conversation with other people, even if they are strangers. A gentle smile can change someone's day.

- **Be real**: We have this concept that being "real" means being raw and uncultured. This does not have to be. People respond well to being real: to talking about different things that come up instead of pretending they don't exist. Being real is who we are, handling issues in right-now reality rather than in the distant past or the ethereal future. Gentleness is how we do it.

- **Refrain from behaving like a know-it-all**: I don't care what your title is, how old you are, how many years you have been saved, how many videos you've watched on social media, or how many books you've read: we are all still learning and developing our faith. None of us has the right to lord what we feel we know over what someone else knows. Listening and correcting in love when it's needed is a sure sign of gentleness.

- **Revive the concept of manners**: Even though I am not a person bound up by traditions, I think that being polite to people, saying "please" and "thank you," addressing others as "sir" or "ma'am," and thinking about the course of polished behavior does a lot to make sure others around us are comfortable and feel a sense of gentle conduct in our actions.

Chapter Ten

Self-Control

IT IS NOT GOOD TO EAT TOO MUCH HONEY,
NOR IS IT HONORABLE TO SEARCH OUT MATTERS THAT ARE TOO DEEP.
LIKE A CITY WHOSE WALLS ARE BROKEN THROUGH
IS A PERSON WHO LACKS SELF-CONTROL.
- PROVERBS 25:27-28

Assignments:
- Read Titus 2:1-8.
- Team up with a small group to maintain greater spiritual connection and accountability.
- Start a new habit (such as exercise or healthy eating) to break a bad habit (such as laziness or poor nutritional choices).

I love God's sense of humor. Anyone who has spent any time walking with God knows that He has a really good sense of humor that starts to seem off-color the second it comes out, in any form, involving us. We're all quick to see it and embrace it when it's about someone else, but the second it comes home to us, we're offended and pout. We can't imagine why God would ever do anything that would seem funny at our expense. It's not really at our expense, it's to teach us something, but at that moment…it seems targeted at us. We never like it, and probably never will. In hindsight, we might laugh, but all too often we still think God was mean and don't understand why God didn't just tell us or outright direct us in some way that would make it seem less hard to swallow.

Well, surprise! The joke's on all of us. God saved the most poorly received fruit for last: the fruit of self-control. Now there's a topic nobody wants to hear about! We want to talk about how we are victims of circumstances, that we can't control our impulses and that nothing we want to do can ever be conquered! We want to believe self-control is impossible and that we really can't stop eating that box of cookies, or over-spending, or control our sexual urges, or what we say to other people…and…and…and we want a recount! Surely God didn't mean that we must be self-controlled and control ourselves, did He?

Actually, that's exactly what God meant. God knew that if we were going to round out the fruit of the Spirit, we needed to hear something that didn't sound polished or super-spiritual or whimsical. It's easy to think that some of the values in the fruit of the Spirit sound so holy, we should sit around wearing white, on a big, puffy cloud, and think about them all day. Of course, this isn't what we should be doing with the fruit of the Spirit, and the fruit of self-control proves this. Self-control is the little reminder that we can decide how we want to behave and that we can do the things that relate to the fruit of the Spirit as we work with God and commit ourselves to the principles contained therein. It doesn't have to be hard, but it does take our own dedication and resolve to move away from the flesh and move closer to God's Spirit.

We can all benefit from study and understanding on self-control and how it can better our lives. Too often we feel like we have failed God in one form or another and that makes us think that we are destined for failure at every turn. Self-control gives us the jolt of reality that even when we've made mistakes – even the biggest imaginable – we can start again, make an effort, and move into greater areas of victory. We do not have to accept defeat, because we really do have the fruit of self-control!

What is self-control?

> **BUD BREAKS: Self-Control**
> #1466 *egkrateia* [eng-krat'-i-ah]: self-control (the virtue of one who masters his desires and passions, esp. his sensual appetites).

Self-control is exactly what it sounds like, which means nothing we discuss in this chapter will be a huge mystery. It's not a fun term with a deep, hidden meaning. Self-control means that an individual is in control of themselves, learning to govern themselves well in a variety of situations that emerge in life. Contrary to what many associate with self-control, it's not all about "sin" (specifically, those of sex or vice). A self-controlled person is self-disciplined, not needing others to hold their hand in guidance and moral teaching. They understand how to assess situations, knowing and recognizing their own limitations and personal temptations. When someone is self-controlled they can, at least somewhat, accept responsibility for their decisions and choices. Contrary to popular belief, being self-controlled isn't a special personality; it is a discipline, one we can all develop through time.

Self-controlled people aren't given to every whim that comes along or every idea that might cross their minds. They recognize there's power in not needing constant supervision and recognize such as an important part of overcoming the temptations of the enemy. Far from being people who are perfect, self-control helps an individual deal with imperfections, all the while growing from glory to glory and faith to faith.

2 Peter 1:-11:

His divine power has given us everything we need for a godly life through our knowledge of Him Who called us by His own glory and goodness. Through these He has given us His very great and precious promises, so that through them you may participate in the divine nature, having escaped the corruption in the world caused by evil desires.

For this very reason, make every effort to add to your faith goodness; and to goodness, knowledge; and to knowledge, self-control; and to self-control, perseverance; and to perseverance, godliness; and to godliness, mutual affection; and to mutual affection, love. For if you possess these qualities in increasing measure, they will keep you from being ineffective and unproductive in your knowledge of our Lord Jesus Christ. But whoever does not have

> **Foundational Fertilizer:** As of the rewrite of this book, I have spent over 25 years in ministry, most of those being full-time ministry. The daily face of ministry is quite different from what we see in the pulpit or a conference. Yes, being in conferences and preaching are wonderful things, but they are not the whole of what goes into the walk and life of a good ministry. I have estimated that approximately 90% of what is done in ministry is never done in the pulpit. Ministers must counsel others, take care of business that applies to churches and ministries, study for lessons and sermons, grow in understanding of the Scriptures, and even more than this. Then, on top of these things, most ministers also have spouses, families, and household duties. The work of ministry reaches a point where it's not all stars and sunshine, and the minister must dedicate themselves to exercising self-control for the things they don't enjoy doing. Not every aspect of ministry is as enjoyable as preaching or fellowshipping with the saints.

them is nearsighted and blind, forgetting that they have been cleansed from their past sins.

Therefore, my brothers and sisters, make every effort to confirm your calling and election. For if you do these things, you will never stumble, and you will receive a rich welcome into the eternal Kingdom of our Lord and Savior Jesus Christ.

- **Self-control recognizes the power God has given us through Jesus Christ**: Jesus tells us in Luke 10:19 that He has given us power. This "power" Jesus talks about is not the power to be a great and mighty ruler over the world's nations, but it gives us spiritual authority. With it, we can be a great and mighty ruler over the most difficult thing we will ever conquer: ourselves. Jesus has given us authority to conquer our challenges and stand victorious over the enemy.

- **Self-control does not work by itself**: Self-control is listed along with faith, goodness, knowledge, perseverance, godliness, mutual affection, and love. If we want to walk in these things, we must have self-control. Nobody wants to be loving or kind to someone who is mean to them. Nobody wants to persevere when it is easier to give up. Self-control works to our benefit to help us walk virtuously when it would be far easier to quit.

- **Self-control helps us be effective and productive**: I decided that when I got to chapter 8 in this book, I wanted to finish it in its entirety the very next day (that being a Tuesday). Even though I made this resolve, it turned out to be a very distracting day. I woke up to a phone call I did not expect, I got an unexpected application for our seminary program, had to take another phone call, one of my dogs had to go to the vet that evening (which created a whole other course of distraction), and distraction after distraction came along to make sure I did not finish this manuscript. I was shocked when first chapter 9 was finished, and I was able to start chapter 10. Despite the distractions, I set myself up to be self-controlled and finish this project. Even when we are distracted or don't feel like doing something, self-control is there to make sure that we finish what we start and do the work we need to do, getting things done in their appointed time.

- **Self-control reminds us we have been cleansed from sin**: Every time we acknowledge we've sinned, it's common to feel like giving up. We can easily assume living in a way that's pleasing to God is impossible. Self-control is God's reminder that we have been cleansed from our past sins and He can forgive our sins now. It also reminds us that we don't have to sin next time (even if we might do so). We can discipline ourselves to follow God's precepts and seek His face in a deeper way.

- **Self-control helps us make our calling and election sure**: People spend their lives searching for the "perfect job," even though there is no such thing. No matter how dedicated you may feel to your calling and election in the beginning, there will be days when what you do is just a "job" to you and isn't very fulfilling. The same is true with spiritual things. Not everything God asks us to do "feels" very fulfilling. Some of the things God asks of us seem very ordinary and boring. These exist to help us develop discipline and purpose in our everyday lives. In order to make our calling and election sure, we must dedicate ourselves via self-control to persevere through the things we don't always enjoy. This brings us to the other side; there, we can understand why God has us do things we don't want to do.

- **Self-control helps keep us from falling**: Some people believe that if you are truly a Christian, it is impossible for you to walk away from God or ever fall into sin. This is a nice idea, but it is not a Biblical one. If self-control exists to help keep us from falling, it is our choice whether to exercise it in our lives. Keeping ourselves disciplined and focused on the right things keeps us from sin and from falling away from God.

The roof on our spiritual house

The last piece of our little spiritual house is the roof. Anyone who has ever had trouble with a roof knows what an important aspect of a home it is. If you have a leak in your roof, it is inevitable to have serious structural damage. You run the risk of winding up with an infestation of insects, destroyed floors, ceilings, rooms, and furniture, and the very expensive repair of replacing the whole roof.

The fruit of self-control is the "roof" of our spiritual house. It needs to remain intact to keep foreign things out and to prevent damage to the rest of the house. If we have a "leak" in our self-control, that can affect our ability to operate in the entire virtue of the fruit of the Spirit. It's essential that self-control is maintained as a priority. It's not mentioned last because it is of no value. If anything, it is mentioned last to remind us that we too play a role in how much we allow or do not allow God to move in our lives. If we want to walk in the fruit of the Spirit, God doesn't take us over by force. We must be self-controlled enough to walk as He asks and move within His call.

Attributes of self-control

Self-control doesn't resemble the stuffy, old librarian who never smiled or had fun that we knew as children. Self-control handles each situation that comes along, echoing the different virtues that have already been discussed in connection with the fruit of the Spirit.

Titus 2:1-2:

You, however, must teach what is appropriate to sound doctrine. Teach the older men to be temperate, worthy of respect, self-controlled, and sound in faith, in love and in endurance.

Titus 2 starts with the oldest first, specifically older men. Even though we are going to look at it from the perspective that the Scriptures provide it, these characteristics are not exclusive to just one specific group of people. One thing about Titus 2 is that it repeats a lot of the same ideas with different age groups (including self-control). This should tell us that different issues (including and especially self-control) are an issue for everyone, at different ages. Whether it's a rough temper or temptations toward certain behaviors that do not represent the conduct God desires us to have, self-control is a discipline for all of them. Whether old or young, we all face – and fight – temptations in our lives.

Older individuals are, I believe, to be models for younger members of the church in how they should conduct themselves and live life. Self-control and temperance (or moderation), self-respecting and thus worthy of respect, and sound in things that pertain to spirituality, all go together. I've met many older people who behaved just as bad (if not worse) than younger people. This is because of a little issue we are calling self-control. No matter how old you are, nobody has the right to behave in a way that discredits God and operates without the good sense to respect other people's boundaries. Self-control reminds us that other people exist in this world, and we do not have the right to intrude upon their space or rights because we want to do something that will affect them.

Titus 2:3-5:

Likewise, teach the older women to be reverent in the way they live, not to be slanderers or addicted to much wine, but to teach what is good. Then they can train the younger women to love their husbands and children, to be self-controlled and pure, to be busy at home, to be kind, and to be subject to their husbands, so that no one will malign the Word of God.

The Bible is no stranger to controversial statements, and various interpretations of Titus 2 often fuels for some controversy. Let us start off by saying that the way Titus 2 is worded is not, by any stretch of the imagination, a justification for abuse or abusive conduct on the part of a spouse. Being abusive is a self-control issue (among other things) and that means such conduct is never, under any circumstances, acceptable. Instead of trying to zero in on one verse taken out of context, if we hear the whole of this passage,

I hear the very same advice given to the older men spoken now to older women, with the same goal: to impact younger generations. Mentioned in context of older women (but applicable to all older people), self-control is essential for role models. Older individuals should be moderate, of good reputation, self-respectable, self-controlled, and teachers of good things. Younger people are encourage to love their families. Does it sound odd to you that loving your spouse and children is addressed here as a matter of self-control? I used to wonder why that was there until I started to consider just what it is like to be a parent, and what a difficult task many spouses and parents face in their everyday lives. Being a spouse and a parent do not equate to a fairy-tale existence. They juggle many duties and responsibilities, and sometimes the people in their atmospheres aren't very lovable. It takes self-control to love a husband when he is busy or having a bad day, and it takes self-control to love children who are making a mess and not doing their chores like they should. It takes self-control to discipline children in a balanced way, without swinging to the extreme of abuse or the extreme of indulgent parenting. It also takes self-control for spouses to avoid temptations (no matter what they might be), to attend to household tasks and chores that need doing, to be kind when you want to scream, and to work in partnership, rather than trying to get your own way all the time. All these things take serious self-discipline. They are not easily achieved without prayer, strong connection to others in the faith, good examples to emulate, and a strong sense of spiritual community.

Titus 2:6-8:

Similarly, encourage the young men to be self-controlled. In everything set them an example by doing what is good. In your teaching show integrity, seriousness and soundness of speech that cannot be condemned, so that those who oppose you may be ashamed because they have nothing bad to say about us.

It may not seem like enough is being said to the young men (especially if you take the advice and literally apply it by gender), but look at this passage, again. We see the command to be self-controlled and the need for them to follow examples, encouraging them to behave with integrity, take their responsibilities and lives

> **POWER POLLINATION:** Titus 2 assigns mentoring work to every age group in the church. The goal is to help others develop greater self-control. What are you doing to help other people develop a greater sense of self-control?

seriously, and to be people who are sound of speech. These things relate not just to the way in which they might handle business, but the way that young spouses with families are also encouraged to handle household issues and handle household relationships. The same issue, repeated, was self-control. This needs to jump out at us in a major way. If we want to have good relationships, good interactions with others, and an overall good sense of relationship with the church and with others in society, we need to be self-controlled.

Temples of the Holy Spirit

The Bible tells us we are "temples of the Holy Spirit." Have you ever stopped to consider what this means? It sounds nice and flowery, something to put in a song, but what it means is actually very important to developing the fruit of self-control in our lives.

1 Corinthians 6:12-20:

"I have the right to do anything," you say — but not everything is beneficial. "I have the right to do anything" — but I will not be mastered by anything. You say, "Food for the stomach and the stomach for food, and God will destroy them both." The body, however, is not meant for sexual immorality but for the Lord, and the Lord for the body. By His power God raised the Lord from the dead, and He will raise us also. Do you not know that your bodies are members of Christ Himself? Shall I then take the members of Christ and unite them with a prostitute? Never! Do you not know that he who unites himself with a prostitute is one with her in body? For it is said, "The two will become one flesh." But whoever is united with the Lord is one with Him in spirit.

Flee from sexual immorality. All other sins a person commits are outside the body, but whoever sins sexually, sins against their own body. Do you not know that your bodies are temples of the Holy Spirit, Who is in you, Whom you have received from God? You are not your own; you were bought at a price. Therefore honor God with your bodies.

There are many different topics discussed here, all of which relate to the Greek culture that surrounded the Corinthian church. Among ancient Greek-influenced culture were a number of different philosophical ideas, which tended to vary in extremes. For example, there were groups that were over-indulgent in eating (Epicureans) and those who believed in required fasts and abstinence (Stoics). The ideas of these groups permeated society, which means they not only influenced those who converted to Christianity, they also influenced Christians, as well. Other issues addressed here include pagan sexual rites (specifically temple prostitution) and sexual immorality. If you mix these seemingly different issues together, they had one thing in common: they either embraced no self-control or an unreasonable denial of it. To find a balancing act, the Apostle Paul reminds believers that they don't house these specific ideas, but the Holy Spirit within them. Thanks to Him, they could avoid being mastered by any set of ideas and devote themselves fully to the work of Christ.

While these specific examples were a direct result of Corinth's cultural scene, these issues relate to us today because they relate to self-control. We may not talk about gluttony often, but we can see it had connection to sexual immorality and pagan rites. Some define gluttony simply as overeating, but I would define it as never having enough of something – whether that "never enough" is food, money, sex, a certain hobby or activity, an item, or something else. Paul clarifies that while everything might be "permitted," everything is not beneficial, no matter what a doctrine may teach. Self-control identifies the difference. If something is going to be harmful, negatively affect our relationship with God, or negatively affect our relationship with other people, we need to consider that it is not beneficial.

We have the witness and discernment to reject things that are sinful or just not beneficial because the Spirit of God is living in us. We are called to honor God with our bodies. This means in many ways our self-control reflects how we care for and treat our bodies, what we use them for, and what we do, because we know we have been bought with a price.

This also raises the issue of the boundaries between self-control and freedom. To many, it seems contradictory to require self-control if we are free. I believe Paul clarifies the issue quite nicely in the passage above. Self-control doesn't mean we are not a free people; it means we know the difference between things that are beneficial and things that are not beneficial. It makes the choice, knowing the sacrifice that has been made, to do what is right. Self-control is still a choice in every situation we face. It is understood that there are many things in this world that seek to control us and use our free agency to make sure nothing has sway or hold over us unto sin, ever again.

Handling temptations

We can't talk about self-control without talking about temptations. If we read the issues present in many New Testament churches, it sounds like the cultures they lived in offered some pretty intense temptations. Every time they went out to the open markets, every time they went in certain stores, every time they were anywhere but at church, they were surrounded by tempting lifestyles, behaviors, indulgences, and yes, sins. If we are objective, we recognize from the words, disciplinary actions, and advice given that the saints of old didn't always reject the temptations they faced.

Now, before we go judging them as "weak," I don't think our culture is much different in some ways than it was back then. For the ancients, their temptations weren't as simple as failing to walk past a strip club without going inside. The idolatrous world that surrounded them impacted their businesses, family lives, and livelihoods. Pagan offerings and practices were attached to every facet of life imaginable. Leaving behind their old ways was not just complicated; it meant they faced constant temptation to return.

Temptations can be as intense for us now as they were then. In modern times, we might face temptations at church as well as away from it! Our workplaces, social lives, and family lives often brim with various temptations. Things that were once regarded as taboo are easy to access now (such as pornography, drugs, alcohol, overspending, etc.). In most instances, when faced with things that tempt us, we don't exercise any more self-restraint than those in New Testament churches did.

The Bible mentions various temptations, and I use some of those to illustrate the point of temptation, but let's not think these are the only temptations that exist. For example, Satan tempted Jesus to turn a stone into bread because He'd been fasting and was hungry. Later, he tried to tempt Him with something a little more relatable to most of us – the authority of the whole world (which Jesus already had!). Temptations are often very personal and very conditional on circumstances. What might tempt me may not tempt you, and what might tempt to the quiet person in the back of the church might be quite different from what tempts the loud person sitting in the second row trying to get the pastor's attention while they preach.

We need to understand that life is full of different temptations. I am not going to talk about avoiding temptations, because I recognize we can't always go out of our way to avoid tempting situations in our lives. While an alcoholic can avoid going to the bar and stay accountable by attending Alcoholics Anonymous meetings, that same alcoholic still must shop at the grocery store where they sell alcohol. It's fine to make better choices in life and avoid places or things that become too tempting, but it's unreasonable to assume we will be able to have a temptation-free life. If we reach the point where we master one temptation, we will, most likely, find ourselves tempted by something else. There's no getting away from it; only learning how to handle it.

There is a good reason why temptation comes up a few times in the New Testament, and why the words surrounding temptation are both strong and disciplining in nature. 1 Corinthians 10:11-13 says:

These things happened to them as examples and were written down as warnings for us, on Whom the culmination of the ages has come. So, if you think you are standing firm, be careful that you don't fall! No temptation has overtaken you except what is common to mankind. And God is faithful: He will not let you be tempted beyond what you can bear. But when you are tempted, He will also provide a way out so that you can endure it.

Matthew 6:13:

*And lead us not into temptation,
but deliver us from the evil one.*

Mark 14:39:

Watch and pray so that you will not fall into temptation. The spirit is willing, but the flesh is weak.

There is no sin in encountering temptation or in being tempted. The Bible even talks of Jesus being tempted (Matthew 4:1-13), and we know He did not sin. This means that even in His moments of temptation, He exercised self-control. Sin only enters the equation if we give in to our temptations and then are controlled by whatever spirit is involved in our sin. Self-control acknowledges the weaknesses we all have, as well as our personal issues. We know our spirits want to please God and do for God, but it will take resolve and self-control to make sure the weaknesses of the flesh do not overtake us. For example, those same men who fell asleep with Jesus in the garden were able to stay up all night to fish. Priorities matter, and self-control is the dividing line for those. I have often said you can starve anything if you don't feed it! In other words, if we do not seek to gratify the impulses and temptations we know lead us into sin long enough, we will starve that nature through self-control and continue to grow spiritually. The only way we can handle temptation is to consistently exercise self-control and deny it.

Don't set yourself up for temptation

In maintaining balance with temptation, we also need to make sure we don't deliberately set ourselves for temptation, to fall into areas of sin. We all need to know our own limits, and our own limits are very personal things. This is an important principle of self-control. Sometimes in an effort to be self-controlled, people will swing to the complete opposite extreme from where they once were. This is not what God asks of us! God encourages us to be balanced and moderate in our lives, not swinging back and forth between extremes. Sometimes our best efforts at what we perceive to be "holy" things are the very things that lead us into temptation the most.

1 Corinthians 7:1-5:

Now for the matters you wrote about: "It is good for a man not to have sexual relations with a woman." But since sexual immorality is occurring, each man should have sexual relations with his own wife, and each woman with her own husband. The husband should fulfill his marital duty to his wife, and likewise the wife to her husband. The wife does not have authority over her own body but yields it to her husband. In the same way, the husband does not have authority over his own body but yields it to his wife. Do not deprive each other except perhaps by mutual consent and for a time, so that you may devote yourselves to prayer. Then come together again so that Satan will not tempt you because of your lack of self-control.

> **PRUNING POINTS:** In what ways are you out of balance in your life? How can you achieve a better balance?

Within the early church, asexuality was often seen as the spiritual ideal. The sexual lasciviousness of Roman and Greek culture left early Christians with the idea that not having sex was more desirable than having it, and that viewpoint led many to think it might be better to abstain from sex all together – even in the case of married couples – than entertain a sexual relationship.

I believe the Corinthians had good intentions when they made their inquiries to the Apostle Paul. Their world was full of temptation, and they were making the effort to do what they thought was the best option. The problem is they were trying to do things according to the flesh, abiding by their own concepts. Through their actions, they were inviting more temptation into their lives. Their level of self-control didn't match their attempts, and even more so, for married couples, it wasn't required.

We too can be like the Corinthians and take this same approach with anything. If we try too hard to over-produce a sense of self-control to look more holy or become more sacrificial, we make more trouble for ourselves. Self-control doesn't exist to be ridiculous in grand gestures so as to feed the temptation to be grandiose and seen by others. Anything – even things that sound good – can feed wrong things within us if we don't aim for balance. That is the goal of self-control, and, in essence, all the fruit of the Spirit. Our purpose in self-control isn't to prove something to others (or even ourselves). God already knows all about us and the only thing He asks us to do is to follow Him faithfully, to the end. If we work toward achieving moderation in our lives, we will accomplish far more than if we keep trying to achieve things by extremes.

Accountability and community

Since the Garden of Eden, God has desired His people to be accountable (Genesis 3:6-19). One of the best ways to achieve greater self-control in life is through community connection. Some people seek to do this through an accountability partner (someone in your life who helps you stay accountable before God), but I believe it is also done through a greater sense of community involvement. We already know we're called to be accountable with our spiritual leaders, but having a good, strong spiritual community in life goes a long way in helping avoid problems before they start. Having friends available for prayer, fellowship, and discussion about anything – even the pitfalls that come with your spiritual walk – is essential.

When it comes to accountability – or the state of being accountable for one's actions before God and others – the issues we face often relate to self-control. Sometimes it's that we are facing temptation, and other times it's that we've given into it. At other times, it's a matter of contemplating options, choices, or admitting to wrongdoing in a given situation. However we recognize such, accountability is part of self-control. When we are able to admit our struggles and things we did wrong or could to better, we go a long way in finding the support we need to stand against temptation in any form that might come along.

A few years back, God showed me that accountability begins long before we fall into situations that are problematic. Most of the time, we don't reveal our failings or shortcomings because we are afraid others will judge us for them. The problem with this is that we don't develop self-control by ourselves, in some sort of vacuum. While this might be a popular message to give, it's not reality. We develop community as we help one another, and we can't help each other if we don't know what's up. We don't have to go through these struggles by ourselves, for two is better than one!

Ecclesiastes 4:9-12:

Two are better than one,
   because they have a good return for their labor:
If either of them falls down,
   One can help the other up.
But pity anyone who falls
   and has no one to help them up.
Also, if two lie down together, they will keep warm.
   But how can one keep warm alone?
Though one may be overpowered,
   two can defend themselves.
A cord of three strands is not quickly broken.

God has put us in a body, the Body of Christ, to help us develop every aspect of the fruit of the Spirit as we keep faith. This includes the fruit of self-control. Whatever you are going through as pertains to self-control, don't feel the need to try and go it alone. Reaching out will help you reach your spiritual goals, because the threefold cord is not easily broken.

> **HAPPY HARVEST:** Self-control has numerous benefits! What benefits of self-control would you like to see manifest in your life?

Producing more excellent fruit

Where are you when it comes to self-control? Where can you do better? Here are some suggestions on ways to produce a more excellent fruit of self-control:

- **Do an honest personal inventory**: The first step to change is to be honest with ourselves. There are all things that we would like to change about ourselves. How can self-control help you achieve some of these changes? Do you want to develop a healthier lifestyle? Quit smoking? Quit drinking? Start exercising? Eat better? Develop a more consistent prayer schedule? Attend church more frequently? Make some new church friends? Join a Bible study group? Consider the different ways that self-control can help you with this process…and then start working on them.

- **Maintain your schedule**: We all know that sometimes things come up that disrupt our schedules and are out of our control, but the point is those disruptions disrupt something established. People used to keep to structure in their lives, because their livelihood depended on it. They got up at a certain time, ate at certain times, worked certain hours, rested certain hours, held to certain hours for leisure time, and slept certain hours. We don't have to be ultra-legalistic about it, but keeping to a certain schedule helps us to be more self-controlled, because we know what we are doing and what needs to be done.

- **Remove the distractions present in your life**: Distractions can be a form of temptation. By focusing on everything around us, we are unable to focus on the task at hand or the assignment at hand, whatever it may be at the time. Self-control doesn't just resist temptation; it also eliminates whatever can be eliminated that can lead to it.

- **Keep a watch on your money**: We don't like to hear it, but many things that tempt our self-control also cost money. We are quick to say we are too poor to pay necessary bills or tithes and offerings, but when a temptation comes knocking, we suddenly have the money. Before the response is, "Don't tell me how to spend my money!" I think it's important to consider that if we pay our necessities first, we won't have as much money left for vices and other things that lead us into sinful actions.

- **Don't let your emotional states get the best of you**: Temptations tend to come into our lives through our emotional states, especially when we are feeling what we often brand as "negative feelings" such as sorrow, loneliness, anger, stress, frustration, or grief. Maintaining good mental and emotional health is a must if we are to exercise good self-control. If remembering difficult feelings do pass isn't enough, there's nothing wrong with seeking out a counselor, talking to a friend or church leader, or getting help to manage your emotional states. When we say don't let your emotions dictate your life, we're not saying deny them. If you need help…get help to manage them.

- **Consider the bigger picture**: Even though it might not feel like it, our lives are bigger than what we are going through right now (even if it seems like we have been stuck where we are for some time). Life is bigger than this feeling, this moment, this temptation, this situation. In the scope of our lives, this one moment does not have to become bigger than one moment, if we are willing to exercise the fruit of self-control.

- **Avoid becoming complacent**: Sometimes we reach a point where we really do believe that things will never change or get better, due to two possibilities: either things have been bad for so long it doesn't seem possible for them to improve, or because we're in a place comfortable enough for us to get by in the long haul. A place of complacency is one of the easiest times for temptation to come in and take over. Rather than grow complacent, take on new challenges that help avoid lazy habits and develop balance within the realm of self-control.

- **Aspire for goals that can be achieved**: Yes, with God all things are possible, and yes we believe that, but I also don't believe that God intends for us to take that to a nonsensical level. You cannot, no matter how much things are possible with God, be in ten different directions at once. You cannot become a neurosurgeon if you have not studied neuroscience. God does not ask that we believe in absurd things that we cannot achieve, because that is just going to lead us into a place where we desire to quit and give up. Self-control is there to discipline us to achieve our goals, one step at a time.

Conclusion

Harvest-Time Reflections

LET YOUR CONVERSATION BE ALWAYS FULL OF GRACE,
SEASONED WITH SALT,
SO THAT YOU MAY KNOW HOW TO ANSWER EVERYONE.
- COLOSSIANS 4:6

When it came to write the final thoughts for this book, what kept coming to my mind was, "be seasoned with salt." I was rather confused by this, because the book itself is not about salt. We're talking about fruit, and I am not one that likes to sprinkle salt on my fruit before I eat it. Returning to our principles of grapes and the vine, it occurred to me that maybe I should look up salt in connection with the winemaking process. It turns out, even amid our fruit, salt is present. In winemaking, the byproduct of the natural tartaric acid is an acidic salt called potassium hydrogen tartrate. It is better known as cream of tartar and is a lesser-known ingredient required in baking. Even the production of the fruit of the vine has a fruit that is used for a completely different purpose. Even in the fruit of the vine, we find salt.

Matthew 5:13-16:

"You are the salt of the earth. But if the salt loses its saltiness, how can it be made salty again? It is no longer good for anything, except to be thrown out and trampled underfoot.

"You are the light of the world. A town built on a hill cannot be hidden. Neither do people light a lamp and put it under a bowl. Instead they put it on its stand, and it gives light to everyone in the house. In the same way, let your light shine before others, that they may see your good deeds and praise your Father in heaven."

- All these wonderful analogies: salt, light, and fruit are given so we can understand the same principle – God wants to do a work within us that is visible to others. It's not just an idea, but something that transforms. The fruit of the Spirit displays the wonderful work the Spirit is doing within you. Having read through this book, and in keeping with the command that we all must become fruit, salt, and light, what can you do better to allow God to develop these essential attributes within you?

- Keep a "fruit journal" for at least 30 days that helps you to identify different aspects of the fruit in your life, in every possible aspect. Look at how well you display fruit, how you can better display fruit, how you receive fruit from others in your life, and areas of life that need fruit!

- Pray for the fruit of the Spirit to manifest in a greater way in your life, calling out each aspect of the fruit by name in prayer.

- Write out a prayer, a poem, an essay, or a song about the fruit of the Spirit. Which aspect speaks to you the most? Why? Which aspect do you need to work on the most?

About the Author

Dr. Lee Ann B. Marino

THESE THAT HAVE TURNED THE WORLD UPSIDE DOWN
ARE COME HITHER ALSO.
- ACTS 17:6 (KJV)

DR. LEE ANN B. MARINO, PH.D., D.MIN., D.D. (she/her) is "everyone's favorite theologian" leading Gen X, Millennials, and Gen Z with expertise in leadership training, queer and feminist theology, general religion, and apostolic theology. She has served in ministry since 1998 and was ordained as a pastor in 2002 and an apostle in 2010. She founded what is now Sanctuary Apostolic Fellowship Empowerment (SAFE) Ministries in 2004. Under her ministry heading  Dr. Marino is founder and Overseer of Sanctuary International Fellowship Tabernacle (SIFT) (the original home of National Coming Out Sunday) and The Sanctuary Network, and Chancellor of Apostolic Covenant Theological Seminary (ACTS).

Affectionately nicknamed "the Spitfire," Dr. Marino has spent over two decades as an "apostle, preacher, and teacher" (2 Timothy 1:11), exercising her personal mandate to become "all things to all people" (1 Corinthians 9:22). Her embrace of spiritual issues (both technical and intimate) has found its home among both seekers and believers, those who desire spiritual answers to today's issues.

Dr. Marino has preached throughout the United States, Puerto Rico, and Europe in hundreds of religious services and experiences throughout the years. A history maker in her own right, she has spent over two decades in advocacy, education, and work for and within minority spiritual communities (including African American, Hispanic, and LGBTQ+). She has also served as the first woman on all-male synods, councils, and panels, as well as the first preacher or speaker welcomed of a different race, sexual orientation, or identity among diverse communities. Today, Dr. Marino's work extends to over 150 countries as she hosts the popular *Kingdom Now* podcast, which is in the top 20 percentile of all podcasts worldwide. She is also the author of over 35 books and the popular Patheos column, *Leadership on Fire*. To date, she has had five bestselling titles within their subject matter: *Understanding*

Demonology, Spiritual Warfare, Healing, and Deliverance: A Manual for the Christian Minister; *Ministry School Boot Camp: Training for Helps Ministries, Appointments, and Beyond*; *Discovering Intimacy: A Journey Through the Song of Solomon*; *Fruit of the Vine: Study and Commentary on the Fruit of the Spirit*; and *Ministering to LGBTQ+ (and Those Who Love Them): A Primer for Queer Theology* (and its accompanying workbook).

As a public icon and social media influencer, Dr. Marino advocates healthy body image (curvy/full-figured), representation as a demisexual/aromantic, and albinism awareness as a model. Known to those she works with, she is a spiritual mom, teacher, leader, professor, confidant, and friend. She continues to transform, receiving new teaching, revelation, and insight in this thing we call "ministry." Through years of spiritual growth and maturity, Dr. Marino stands as herself, here to present what God has given to her for any who have an ear to hear.

For more information, visit her website at kingdompowernow.org.

www.ingramcontent.com/pod-product-compliance
Lightning Source LLC
LaVergne TN
LVHW051114080426
835510LV00018B/2041